Mystical Women, Mystical Body

Mystical Women
Mystical Body

Owen F. Cummings

PASTORAL PRESS
PORTLAND · OREGON

Cover: *Christ Our Mother*

Julian of Norwich wrote, "A mother can lay her child tenderly on her breast, but our kind Mother Jesus can lead us easily into his blessed breast through his dear open side, showing us there part of the godhead and joys of heaven with the inner sureness of endless bliss."

Artwork © 2000 Steve Erspamer, S.M. Used with permission. All rights reserved.

Dedication page illustration by Susan Cummings of an icon originally directed by Hildegard of Bingen: *Imago muliebris,* see *Scivias* 6:2, Plate 15.

Page 101, photo of Thérèse of Lisieux © Office Central de Lisieux, Maison d'édition du Carmel, France. Used with permission. All rights reserved.

Page 102, photo of Edith Stein © Edith Stein Archiv, American Office, Carmelite Monastery, Elysburg, Pennsylvania. Used with permission. All rights reserved.

ISBN 1-56929-036-9

© 2000 Pastoral Press
A Division of OCP Publications
5536 N.E. Hassalo
Portland, OR 97213
Phone: 800-LITURGY (548-8749)
Email: liturgy@ocp.org
Web site: www.pastoralpress.com
Web site: www.ocp.org

Library of Congress Cataloging-in-Publication Data

Cummings, Owen F.
    Mystical women, mystical body/Owen Cummings.
        p. cm.
    Includes bibliographical references and index.
    ISBN 1-56929-036-9 (pbk.)
        1. Women mystics. 2. Lord's Supper—History. 3. Mysticism. 4. Lord's Supper—Catholic
Church. 5. Catholic Church—Doctrines—History. I. Title.

BV5095.A1 C86 2000
248.2'2'082—dc21   00-033963

To my daughters

Anne Catherine

Susan Carol

Mary Elizabeth Margaret

Contents

Introduction

Many textbooks on eucharistic theology fail to take seriously both mysticism and the experience and reflection of women. These omissions do not necessarily detract from the high quality of what is presented, but without attempting to gild the lily, as it were, the inclusion of mysticism and women's eucharistic experience and reflection can offer a further richness to what is already in the textbooks. In recent times much solid work has been done on these two topics. Inaccessible mystical writings have been made more easily available in English,[1] and careful historical work on the experience of Christian women by scholars such as Caroline Walker Bynum has done much to shed light on what has been a little appreciated aspect of Christian theology.[2] These studies have yet to make their way into the doctrinal literature on the Eucharist. This book is a modest and popular contribution in that direction.

Take, for example, the excellent study by the Irish systematic theologian and my own teacher, Raymond Moloney, S.J., in his *The Eucharist*.[3] Few studies have been as thoroughly informed as Moloney's, both in biblical-historical and systematic terms, yet a cursory consultation with the general index establishes that the only mystical woman mentioned with respect to the Eucharist is Therese of Lisieux. Only four other women are mentioned in the book: Aileen Guilding and Annie Jaubert, both biblical scholars, Frances M. Young, the New Testament and patristic specialist, and Evelyn Underhill, the Anglican spiritual writer. This seems a pity, given the range of women's eucharistic experience and reflection that is to be found throughout the last millennium. When it comes to mysticism,

1

Moloney writes: "The great saints and mystics sometimes leave us breathless with their accounts of what the Eucharist has come to mean for them."[4] After mentioning Therese of Lisieux, he goes on to provide examples from Cyril of Alexandria, Hilary of Poitiers, Henry Suso, Jan van Ruysbroeck and the founder of his own religious congregation, Ignatius Loyola — a fine beginning, surely, but there are so many more, including many more women.

Among the various reasons one might give for these omissions, three stand out as in need of comment. The first and perhaps most obvious reason has to do with the fact that most Christian theology has been written by men. This is obvious from the cultures and contexts of the past two thousand years. While it is true that in the millennium that has just come to a close the names of more women appear in the theological records, nevertheless the writing and teaching of theology have been male-dominated activities until relatively recently. Secondly, the language of mysticism is much less cautious and controlled than that of scientific theology. Louis K. Dupre remarks, "Language, especially language about the ineffable, never copies; it always creates."[5] This is the way of the mystics. If mystical language is always creative, not imitative, then it becomes difficult for systematic theologians to accommodate it within their "systems." The language eludes and exceeds systematic elaboration, and so tends not to be incorporated into theological syntheses. The third reason is related. Much modern theology has been removed from the Church to the academy, from the living and worshiping community to the lecture room. This is both gain and loss. It is gain insofar as theology has benefited from the finely tuned techniques and methodologies of the academic world. One thinks of the contemporary approaches to Scripture, the writing of Church history and the stimulus given to theology through interaction with modern and contemporary philosophies. It is also loss. If theology is "faith seeking understanding," in Saint Anselm's famous description, then the practice of theology outside the school of the Church, which is the primary mediator of faith, can only be loss. All of the mystical women treated here belong within the Church, not the academy, with the possible exception of Edith Stein. Paradoxically, in our times the writings of these women mystics are being studied as much in the academy as in the Church. In this book, however, the people of the Church are being invited to taste and sample some of the wisdom of their holy women.

This wisdom is from the "Mystical Body" and about the "Mystical Body." Any separation of the Eucharist and the Church can only lead to the impoverishment of both. In modern Catholicism we tend to think of the "Mystical Body of Christ" as the Church, and the Eucharist as the "real Body of Christ," so that the one and the other are entirely discrete and distinct. This is not the larger tradition of the Church. Henri de Lubac, S.J., wrote in 1944: "In the thought of all Christian antiquity Eucharist and Church are linked together. The relationship gets a very special emphasis in the writings of Saint Augustine, and the same is true of the Latin authors of the seventh, eighth and ninth centuries."[6] The necessary interplay between the Eucharist and the Church forms the backdrop to all the women studied here. These women did not go to the theological schools of Europe, to Paris, Oxford, Bologna, but they had imbibed this insight that the Eucharist makes the Church, that the Body of Christ is for the Body of Christ — hence the title of this book, *Mystical Women, Mystical Body.* The title is intended to point up the connection between the eucharistic Body of Christ and the ecclesial Body of Christ.

Each chapter deals briefly with the life and context of the subject, moves on to a brief appreciation of her theology/ spirituality, and then deals with her eucharistic reflection and appreciation.

Recently I was asked why I spend so much time researching the Church's tradition of reflection on the Eucharist instead of engaging with central, contemporary eucharistic concerns, for example, communion services in the absence of a priest. Given the declining number of priests, surely this is a more pressing issue for engagement and analysis than looking into an ecclesial past that is gone forever. This impatience with historical theology is a position with which I find myself in disagreement. Tradition is nothing other than the Church perpetuating herself until the *parousia*, the consummation of all things in Christ. It seems to me impossible to perpetuate ourselves as Church unless we know who we are, and it seems impossible to know who we are without some informed grasp of who we have been. Our foremothers and forefathers in the Christian faith strove and struggled to hand on to their children the precious gift of faith they had received. If we would do the same for our children, then we must grapple to understand their appreciation of the faith; and the very grappling itself is rewarding, as we find ourselves enriched by their vision.

[1] See, for example, the series, The Classics of Western Spirituality: A Library of the Great Spiritual Masters, Mahwah NJ: Paulist Press.

[2] The following titles give some indication of Bynum's ongoing and important research in this area: *Jesus as Mother: Studies in the Spirituality of the High Middle Ages,* Berkeley: University of California Press, 1982; *Holy Feast and Holy Fast: The Religious Significance of Food to Medieval Women,* Berkeley: University of California Press, 1987; *Fragmentation and Redemption: Essays on Gender and the Human Body in Medieval Religion,* New York: Zone Books, 1991.

[3] Collegeville MN: The Liturgical Press, 1995.

[4] Ibid., p. 251.

[5] *Religious Mystery and Rational Reflection,* Grand Rapids MI: William B. Eerdmans, 1998, p. 119.

[6] *Corpus Mysterium,* Paris: Aubier, 1944, p. 23.

Chapter 1

Hildegard of Bingen

Saint Hildegard of Bingen (1098–1179), founder and first abbess of the Benedictine community of Bingen, often described as the "Sybil of the Rhine," was the last of ten children in a noble family of Bermersheim near Alzey.[1] Her parents, Hildebert and Mechthild, as a pious act gave over their eight-year-old daughter to an aristocratic hermit named Jutta, under whose tutelage Hildegard learned to read the Latin Bible and to chant the monastic office. Other women joined them and they formed a Benedictine abbey. When Jutta died in 1136 Hildegard was elected abbess.

In 1141 she received the prophetic call, her awareness of a special vocation from God, that in time led to the composition of her most famous work, the *Scivias* (The title *Scivias* is an abbreviation of the Latin phrase *Scito Vias Domini,* "Know the ways of the Lord."), and to enter upon her public mission. According to her official biography, Hildegard experienced visions from her early childhood, described by Barbara Newman as follows: "She could see things that were invisible to those around her; she foretold the future; and her visual field was filled at all times with a strange luminosity that she later came to call 'the reflection of the living Light' . . . Finally, on rare occasions she came into contact with a greater brightness, which she called 'the living Light' itself; her description of this experience (written at the age of 77) suggests a direct encounter with the divine presence."[2]

It was, however, the prophetic call of 1141 that enabled Hildegard to understand these visions of many years as instruments of divine revelation. It took her a further ten years to put the *Scivias* into writing, aided by two close friends: Pope Eugene III, a disciple of Saint Bernard of

Hildegard of Bingen

Clairvaux, acquired through him a copy of the *Scivias* and read it publicly at the Synod of Trier (1147–1148). For this reason Hildegard and her vision received the seal of papal approval, ensuring its ecclesial reception. Having been one of Bernard's monks, Eugene was an ardent reformer who tried to raise clerical and monastic standards. For this reason, he held a series of important synods at Paris (April–June 1147), Trier (winter 1147–1148, the synod at which Hildegard's *Scivias* was read) and Rheims (March 1148).

About this time Hildegard received a vision in which she was instructed to establish a new convent near Bingen. Acting upon the vision, she met with opposition both inside and outside the convent, and she spent the 1150s maintaining and developing the security of her new establishment. The new foundation, the Rupertsberg, quickly became a center of pilgrimage as a result of Hildegard's growing fame. During that same difficult decade, she also wrote two scientific works and kept up a voluminous correspondence with clergy, religious and secular rulers as well as ordinary women and men. With seemingly indefatigable energy, in 1158 Hildegard set about three major preaching tours focused on the renewal of the Church, and during this period also composed a further visionary work with the title *Book of Life's Merits*.

In 1163, at the request of the canons of Mainz, she wrote against the Cathari (the "Purists"), a medieval, dualistic sect thoroughly critical of the Church, who were making numerous converts in the Rhineland by the 1160s. One historian of heresy has described the Cathari in these words: "[They] became too numerous to be tolerated. . . . They were found mainly in the cities. The reason for their success was that the orthodox Church was weak, its clergy mostly ignorant, luxurious, corrupt, indolent and profane. . . . Simony and concubinage were rife. . . . [The Cathari] attracted the idealistic in an age when there was much yearning for spiritual fulfillment, exemplified by the orthodox movements which gave birth to the Cistercians, Dominicans and Franciscans."[3] As part of their dualist vision of reality, they were opposed to the sacraments of marriage and the Eucharist. Hildegard, a kindred reforming spirit, would have been sympathetic with their reforming ideals to some degree, but certainly not with their anti-institutional and anti-sacramental bias. Her constant emphasis in the *Scivias* that God in Christ becomes flesh and food in the Eucharist probably stems from her anti-Cathari stance.[4]

Her last visionary work, *Book of Divine Works*, which is marked by a powerful sense of the Divine Love, sets out her mature understanding of history and the last things.

The *Scivias*

The *Scivias* may be read not only as a visionary text but also as a *summa* of Christian doctrine, a literary form that was beginning to flourish at this time. Barbara Newman notes, "If Hildegard had been a male theologian, her *Scivias* would undoubtedly have been considered one of the most important of the early medieval *summas.*"[5] The book was addressed mainly to the clergy, monks and theologians of her day, summoning them to reform and repentance; this accounts for the interest in and the endorsement of the work by Pope Eugene. At the beginning of Book 1, Vision 1, of the *Scivias*, Hildegard heard God commission her:

> Cry out and speak of the origin of pure salvation until those people are instructed, who, though they see the inmost contents of the Scriptures, do not wish to tell them or preach them, because they are lukewarm and sluggish in serving God's justice. Unlock for them the enclosure of mysteries that they, timid as they are, conceal in a hidden and fruitless field. Burst forth into a fountain of abundance and overflow with mystical knowledge, until they who now think you contemptible because of Eve's transgression are stirred up by the flood of your irrigation. For you have received your profound insight not from humans, but from the lofty

and tremendous Judge on high, where this calm-
ness will shine strongly with glorious light among
the shining ones.

Because Hildegard was a woman, "because of Eve's trans-
gression," some would castigate her for teaching and preaching. This was not to hold her back, according to her visions,
for the insight she has received had come from God. It was as
if she sensed that the laity experience a real need for a more
profound immersion in theology; the *Scivias* was a clarion call
to the clergy to wake up to that fact and to meet that need.
About 1290 the medieval Parisian theologian, Henry of Ghent,
raised the question whether a woman could be a doctor of theology. There was a minimal sense in which women might be
able to teach theology, according to Henry, but it should be
done privately, not in public before the Church, and it should
be restricted to other women and girls.[6] Such sentiments give
us some small clue about the innovation of Hildegard's teaching and preaching role in her society.

Each vision of the *Scivias* shares a uniform structure. First,
Hildegard begins with a straightforward and brief account of
what she has seen, at the end of which comes a formula, "And I
heard a voice from heaven, saying. . . . " Now the vision becomes
a sort of text, somewhat like Holy Scripture, that requires her
interpretation and comment to render its meaning clear.[7] The
text of the *Scivias* is divided into three books: Book One, "The
Creator and Creation"; Book Two, "The Redeemer and
Redemption"; and Book Three, "The History of Salvation
Symbolized by a Building." Our concern is with the second
vision in which Hildegard presents her sacramental theology.

The Eucharist

The section of Book Two of the *Scivias* that presents
Hildegard's eucharistic doctrine is entitled "Christ's Sacrifice
and the Church"; it is the longest of the visions. In Vision Six,
as she elucidates "Christ's Sacrifice and the Church," she follows what had become a standard patristic way of comment-

ing on eucharistic belief and theology, that is, by commenting on individual parts of the rite of the Eucharist. This is the approach found, for example, in Cyril of Jerusalem's *Lectures on the Christian Sacraments* (d. c. 386). Cyril comments on the meaning of the priest's hand-washing, the holy kiss of peace, the eucharistic prayer, the Lord's Prayer and holy communion itself.[8] In similar fashion, Hildegard takes up the following themes and aspects of the rite: the ecclesiological basis for the Eucharist, the approach of the priest to the altar, the Father's remembrance of the Passion of Christ, why bread and wine are offered, the consecration, the distribution of communion, the effects of communion and the different states of those who communicate. This list of topics is not exhaustive, but gives a good sense of Hildegard's approach.

There is what can only be described as a eucharistic ecclesiology in Hildegard's vision, but one with its own particular shape. Normally, one would take as the hallmark of eucharistic ecclesiology the idea that "the Eucharist makes the Church." Hildegard has this idea, but gives her own representation of it:

> And after these things, I saw the Son of God hanging on the cross, and the aforementioned image of a woman coming forth like a bright radiance from the ancient counsel. By divine power she was led to Him, and raised herself upward so that she was sprinkled by the blood from his side; and thus, by the will of the Heavenly Father, she was joined with Him in happy betrothal and nobly dowered with his body and blood.[9]

The Church is imaged as a bride prepared for marriage to her husband. Christ crucified is the husband of the Church, and Lady Church's dowry is his body and blood. Every time the Eucharist is celebrated, this event is remembered by the Father as the dowry of Lady Church is shown to him: "And as that image grew in strength, I saw an altar, which she frequently approached, and there each time looked devotedly at her dowry and modestly showed it to the Heavenly Father and His angels."[10]

This vision is beautifully captured in a miniature painted under Hildegard's own direction, expressing succinctly her eucharistic ecclesiology. There is an upper and a lower picture in the miniature. In the upper picture, Christ is depicted on the cross, with Lady Church close by him so that some of his blood flows on to her and some into the chalice which she is holding. In the lower picture Lady Church kneels before the altar for the celebration of the Eucharist, with her out-stretched hands pointing toward the chalice containing the blood of Christ, that is, her dowry. The upper picture is con-nected to the lower by fire reaching from the cross to the altar. In the vision, Christ and Lady Church become ontologically one through the Eucharist, but the Eucharist understood as dowry. Here in medieval dress and under the image of mar-riage, the indissoluble union of Christ and Church are affirmed. This is eucharistic ecclesiology. It is all God's work for human salvation.

Hildegard comments on the vision, this woman coming forth from the brightness of the divine radiance: "When the inno-cent Lamb was lifted up on the altar of the cross for human salvation, the Church suddenly appeared in Heaven by a pro-found mystery . . . and by the Supreme Majesty she was joined to the Only-Begotten Son of God."[11] This Bride of Christ now becomes a mother, Lady Church becomes Mother Church, giv-ing birth to her children:

> As a bride, subjected to her bridegroom in her offering of subordination and obedience, receives from him a gift of fertility and a pact of love for procreating children, and educates them as to their inheritance, so too the Church, joined to the Son of God in the exercise of humility and charity, receives from Him the regeneration of the Spirit

and water to save souls and restore life, and sends those souls to Heaven. . . . She is nobly dowered with His body and blood; for the Only-Begotten of God conferred His body and blood in surpassing glory on His faithful, who are the Church and her children, that through Him they may have life in the celestial city.[12]

Christ and Mother Church bring children to the life that is eternal, the eschatological life of heaven.

Underlying this nuptial image is a deep sense of the eucharistic presence of Christ. However, Hildegard does not lose sight of the trinitarian dimension of this presence. She writes, using the analogy of the gold-refiner:

As the goldsmith first unites his gold by melting it in the fire, and then divides it when it is united, so I, the Father, first glorify the body and blood of My Son by the sanctification of the Holy Spirit when it is offered, and then, when it is glorified, distribute it to the faithful for their salvation.[13]

Her way of speaking here, "The sanctification of the Holy Spirit," suggests an epiclesis, thus avoiding any narrowly reductionist approach to the consecration and making the trinitarian movement of the Eucharist more explicit. She considers this trinitarian dimension later in Vision Six when she associates the Eucharist with the Son's mission from the Father. It all fits in an integrated way as the Father through the Son fashions the mechanism of the Eucharist to bring all humanity to himself:

For as wine flows out of the vine, so My Son went forth from My heart; and My Only-Begotten too was the true Vine, and many branches went forth from Him, for in Him the faithful have been planted who through His Incarnation are fruitful in good works . . . As He came sweetly forth from the heart of His Father, He now sweetly displays His blood as wine; and as he was miraculously born of the Virgin, so His body is miraculously manifested in bread, for He is the cluster of grapes that will never suffer defect or loss.[14]

Anselm of Canterbury's (c.1033–1109) treatise, *Why God Became Man,* described Christ's death on the cross as an act of satisfaction; it is difficult to know how quickly it became available and took hold, but there is none of it in this expression of Hildegard's. On the contrary, the mystery of redemption flows from the heart of the Father to draw humanity into that heart through the Eucharist. Barbara Newman rightly comments about this emphasis of Hildegard: "This is an essentially Eastern theology of the Eucharist, sacramental rather than sacrificial in its emphasis. Once again not the cross but the Incarnation provides the focal point of devotion."[15]

To further her understanding of the eucharistic presence of Christ Hildegard draws a parallel between the transformation of the eucharistic gifts and the mysteries of the annunciation and incarnation.

> The Blessed Virgin heard true words of consolation from the angel in secret, and believed . . . and said, "Behold the handmaid of the Lord: be it unto me according to your word." . . . The priest . . . offering Almighty God in devotion of heart speaks the words of salvation in the service of humility: then the Supernal Majesty will receive this oblation and transmute it with miraculous power into the body and blood of the Holy Redeemer. How? As My Son miraculously received humanity in the Virgin so now this oblation miraculously becomes His body and blood on the altar.[16]

In one of her letters Hildegard states the parallel even more clearly: "That same power of the Most High which formed flesh in the Virgin's womb changes the oblation of bread and wine on the altar into the sacrament of flesh and blood, brooding over it with his power, at the words of the priest."[17] The force of this parallel suggests unmistakably that Hildegard's teaching is "in essence identical with the doctrine later defined by Fourth Lateran and elaborated by Thomas Aquinas."[18] In other words, Hildegard is teaching the mystery of Christ's eucharistic presence in the same doctrinally sound way, but without the term *transubstantiation*. Also, the parallel portrays a Marian image of the priest. As Mary became the instrument of the real presence of Christ in her womb, so also the priest at Mass becomes the instrument of the real presence of Christ also. As Barbara Newman puts it, "In a more personal way, [Mary] is also the paradigm of every priest who confects that body."[19]

As a consequence of receiving this Christ, really present in the eucharistic gifts, the Christian achieves a profound union with Christ, so that Christ is with and in those who receive him. This alters the face of human suffering, which now takes on what might be called a "Christic" aspect:

> And then for My name's sake you will endure many tribulations, and I will endure them with you; not because I will suffer any miseries in the body after this, as I did when I was in the world in the body, but because you will endure them in My name. Therefore I will endure them with you, since you are in Me and I am in you.[20]

The reality of evil and suffering in life is not erased but, in this eucharistic vision and expression of Hildegard's, evil and suffering cease to be philosophical problems to be solved through human ratiocination; they become a Christian mystery to be entered into and to be lived.

It is sometimes claimed that as the eucharistic controversies of the Middle Ages developed, the eschatological dimension of the Eucharist fell into the background. There is some truth to this, but certainly one can still see the eschatological aspect in Hildegard. "[Christ's] body and blood must be worshipped in the Church in a true service," she maintains, "until the last person to be saved by the mystery appears at the end of the world . . . (and thus, humanity will) attain to the banquet of eternal beatitude."[21]

The Fourth Lateran Council in 1215 was to mandate annual communion for Christians. Writing some sixty years earlier, Hildegard insists upon communion under both kinds: "But let not anyone who receives this sacred flesh refuse to take the blood of the mystery too; for My Son is pure above all things and a mirror of virtue, and so His noble blood must be received."[22] She is equally insistent that, in this sacrament, not quantity but holiness must be considered: "But let those who receive this sacrament in greater or lesser quantity understand that the receivers of more and of less have received the same amount of power, for the sacrament consists not in quantity but in holiness. It saves those who receive according to their faith. . . ."[23] The dispositions of the recipient may not be neglected in holy communion; quality of reception, not quantity, is what counts. Her eucharistic theology is very balanced, with neither sacramental magic nor automatism. At the same time, she is most respectful of the details of the rite, which may not simply be disregarded at the whim of the celebrant:

> One who unknowingly does something wrong in forgetful neglect as to vestments or words pertaining to this office must be corrected by a severe and salutary penance; but if he seeks My mercy he shall find it, for he did not perpetrate the transgression voluntarily in malice of heart. But if one transgresses knowingly in these sacramental rites, either from mental apathy or from wickedness of heart, I will be offended. . . .[24]

It is comforting to know that the liturgical entrepreneur existed before Vatican Council II.

Hildegard of Bingen

Toward the end of the section of her vision on the Eucharist, Hildegard comments on the five states of communicants.[25] First are those "who are bright of body and fiery of soul." These are the people who have a true and faithful recognition that the sacrament is the body and blood of Christ. Second are those "who are pale of body and shadowed in soul." They lack firm belief in the sacrament, perhaps entertaining some doubt or other. Third come the sinners, "who seem hairy in body and dirty in soul." Contaminated by serious sin, they should have attended to the Sacrament of Penance before receiving communion. Then there are the people "surrounded in body by sharp thorns and leprous of soul," people marked by anger, hate and envy. The fifth state consists of "those bloody in body and foul as a decayed corpse in soul." Hildegard says that such "make divisions among people with bloody hands and render their souls foul with the putrefying corruption of cruel wickedness . . ." The most obvious way of making sense of this group is to understand them as people who split the communion of the Church, in the manner described by Paul in 1 Corinthians, people who for whatever reason seem to delight in splitting up into competing factions the one body of Christ. Those who are not worthy to receive the sacrament should mend their ways, confess their sins and return to the banquet of life.

Finally, Hildegard warns that Christians should avoid eucharistic rationalism:

> But if you, O human, say to yourself in your vacillating heart, "How did the oblation on the altar become the body and blood of God's Son?" I will answer you: Why, O human, do you ask this, and for what purpose do you enquire about it? Do I require you to know it? Why do you peer into my secrets about the body and blood of My Son? You should not seek out these things, but only keep them diligently and accept them in fear and veneration.[26]

The ninth century had witnessed the first attempts in the history of Christian theology at presenting a systematic and comprehensive study of the Eucharist. Crude, physicalist approaches existed alongside what seemed like mere symbolical approaches to Christ's eucharistic presence.[27] Lateran Council IV (1215) had not yet formally introduced the term *transubstantiation* into ecclesial language. Hildegard may have recognized a danger in the eucharistic probings of some of her peers and approaches the gift of the Eucharist with unquestioning faith.

Conclusion

In order to grow eucharistically in Christian life, it is important to be both enriched and challenged by the treasure of the Church's tradition. Hildegard of Bingen's reflections on the Eucharist both enrich and challenge contemporary Catholics. The enrichment consists in a deep vein of monastic eucharistic theology, in contrast to scholastic eucharistic theology. We are so used to associating the Middle Ages with scholasticism, with the scientific and academic theology of the great schools of Paris, Oxford, Bologna, that we miss the trees for the forest, so to speak. Without detracting from the achievements of the scholastics, we need also to be enriched by the no less valuable contribution of monastic theology with its biblical commentary, doctrinal teaching and mystical appropriation. Hildegard of Bingen is an outstanding exemplar of monastic theology. Her eucharistic theology has a vitality that one does not always find in the formal treatises. The challenge comes in Hildegard's panoramic vision of the Christian mysteries carefully worked together, especially Trinity-Cross-Church-Eucharist, her easy and unforced use of feminine and maternal images to speak of the deep things of faith and her non-ideological sense of eucharistic balance. In a Church in which ideology, polarization and alienation occur all too frequently, perhaps the witness of this twelfth century woman is a challenge that we neglect at great loss to ourselves.

---

[1] I am indebted to the excellent account of Barbara Newman in her "Introduction," in *Hildegard of Bingen, Scivias,* translated by Mother Columba Hart and Jane Bishop, introduced by Barbara J. Newman, preface by Caroline Walker Bynum, New York-Mahwah: Paulist Press, 1990, pp. 9–53, referred to henceforth in this way: Newman, "Introduction."

Hildegard of Bingen

2 Ibid., p. 11.

3 David Christie-Murray, *A History of Heresy,* Oxford and New York: Oxford University Press, 1976, p. 105.

4 Caroline Walker Bynum, *Holy Feast and Holy Fast: The Religious Significance of Food to Medieval Women,* Berkeley-Los Angeles-London: University of California Press, 1987, p. 252.

5 Newman, "Introduction," p. 23.

6 Bernard McGinn, "Introduction," in Bernard McGinn, ed., *Meister Eckhart and the Beguine Mystics,* New York: The Continuum Publishing Company, 1994, p. 1. See also the very fine essay of Hugh Feiss, O.S.B., "Hildegard's Vision of the Eucharist (*Scivias* 2.6): Theology and Pastoral Practice," *The American Benedictine Review,* 49, 1998, pp. 166–67.

7 Newman, "Introduction," p. 22.

8 Frank L. Cross, ed., *St. Cyril of Jerusalem's Lectures on the Sacraments,* London: S.P.C.K., 1951, pp. 71–80.

9 *Scivias,* 2.6, p. 237. Feiss, op. cit., p. 169 writes: "If one were to describe (the vision of *Scivias* 2.6) in contemporary theological terms, one might call this vision: 'Eucharist-Centered Ecclesiology as the Basis for the Sacramental Ministry of the Good Pastor.' By 'Eucharist-centered ecclesiology' is meant an understanding of the church which flows from the celebration of the Eucharist." It is gratifying and supportive to find an acknowledged expert in medieval theology recognizing eucharistic ecclesiology in Hildegard.

10 *Scivias,* 2.6, p. 237.

11 Ibid., 2.6.1, p. 238.

12 Ibid., pp. 238–239.

13 Ibid., 2.6.5, p. 240.

14 Ibid., 2.6.28–29, pp. 255–56.

15 Barbara Newman, *Sister of Wisdom: St. Hildegard's Theology of the Feminine,* Berkeley-Los Angeles: University of California Press, 1987, p. 191.

16 *Scivias,* 2.6.15, p. 246.

17 Letter 43, cited in Newman, *Sister of Wisdom,* p. 190. Stating that "We know that Hildegard was aware of current theological thinking about the Eucharist," Feiss, op. cit., p. 172–73, goes on to make reference to the pre-Lateran IV eucharistic debates. See Owen F. Cummings, *Eucharistic Soundings,* Dublin: Veritas Publications, 1999, pp. 30–40.

18 Newman, "Introduction," p. 33. Feiss, op. cit., pp. 179–80, points out the rich vocabulary of Hildegard for the transformation of the eucharistic gifts, and that she uses the adverb "transubstantially" in Letter 47.

19 *Sister of Wisdom,* p. 194. See also the reflections of Walker Bynum, op. cit., pp. 264–65.

20 *Scivias,* 2.6.22, p. 251.

21 Ibid., 2.6.24, 27, pp. 252, 255.

22 Ibid., 2.6.46, p. 264.

23 Ibid., 2.6.41, p. 262.

24 Ibid., 2.6.48, pp. 264–65.

25 Ibid., 2.6.51–57, pp. 266–68.

26 Ibid., 2.6.60, p. 270.

27 A clear and straightforward overview of this complex period may be found in David N. Bell, *Many Mansions: An Introduction to the Development and Diversity of Medieval Theology, West and East,* Kalamazoo MI: Cistercian Publications, 1996, pp. 285–304.

Chapter 2

Hadewijch of Antwerp

In medieval Europe there emerged communities of women known as Beguines, who lived pious and devout lives, sometimes on their own, sometimes in small communities. They prayed in common, engaged in charitable works and made a promise of celibacy and obedience to a rule while they were Beguines but retained the use of private property and could, if they desired, change their status and marry. Their intense and profound spirituality made them on the one hand different from nuns, and on the other different from ordinary laywomen. As they were not structured into the institutional life of the Church, this gave rise to suspicion and problems. As Dennis Devlin puts it, "The lack of ecclesiastical discipline and official hierarchical approval proved threatening in [the] public phase of the Beguine movement."[1] Blessed Hadewijch of Antwerp was probably a Beguine.

Little is known about Hadewijch (Dutch for Hedwig) because, unlike Hildegard of Bingen, no official biography of her was written by a contemporary or near contemporary and because as a Beguine she did not live in a monastery where a tradition of biography existed. This "first great poet in the Flemish language" probably wrote between 1220 and 1240.[2] Hadewijch's works survive in only four manuscripts and were not well known until they were rediscovered in the nineteenth century by some medievalists.[3] What little we know of her has to be gathered from her letters and poems, in the small hints of self-revelation that they afford.

Hadewijch seems to have been the mistress or guide to a group of Beguines whom she addresses authoritatively.[4] In Vision 1 the angel addresses her in these words: "O mistress, you climb this tree from the beginning to the end, all the way to the profound roots of the incomprehensible God!"[5] The term "mistress" suggests that Hadewijch was the leading light and guide of this community of Beguines. Despite their commitment and spiritual aspirations, the Beguines appear to have resented Hadewijch's leadership. She seems to have experienced opposition both inside and outside her community, based on the angel's address to her in Vision 4, "You, unknown to all your friends and to all your enemies!"[6] The forces of opposition seem to have been successful, as she was separated from her companions and accused of teaching a form of quietism, that is, the annihilation of all human desires in the spiritual life so that an utterly disinterested love of God might flourish. In one of her letters addressed to her anonymous Beguine companion and to be shared with her friends Sara, Emma and Margriet, Hadewijch spoke of herself as being "in this life of exile."[7] Summing up the consensus of scholarship, Mother Columba Hart, O.S.B., concludes: "The general opinion of scholars at present seems to be that Hadewijch actually was evicted from her Beguine community and exiled; that she was made the talk of the town . . . and thrown out because of her doctrine that one must live Love."[8] Because she spoke often of caring for the sick, and urged this charitable work on her Beguines, scholars speculate that after her eviction from the community she may have offered her services to a hospital for the poor, which would have afforded her access to the hospital's chapel.[9]

She was well educated, being versed in the Latin Bible, theology and the liberal arts disciplines of the day, including the French language. Saint Augustine was the only non-biblical saint to appear to her in her visions, so we may surmise that she had a special devotion to him, undoubtedly because of his love for the Trinity. He is described as "St. Augustine, who was old and perfect in the love of our Beloved."[10] One commentator describes Hadewijch as having "an astonishing degree of culture, both profane and theological."[11] Hadewijch composed poems, visions and letters, now available in English in a translation by Hart.[12]

Eucharistic Vision

Dennis Devlin writes about the Beguines, "While Beguines and Cistercian nuns had in common certain devotional interests and shared the same mystical inclinations, there was one devotional theme much more strongly associated with the Beguines. This was devotion to the Eucharist, especially to the real presence of the human Christ."[13] First, let us sketch briefly Hadewijch's mystical background.

Hadewijch was first and foremost a mystic of Love, whose great twelfth century master was Saint Bernard of Clairvaux (1090–1153); his thought was mediated to her through the treatises of Bernard's friend and interpreter, William of St. Thierry (c.1085–1148).[14] This notion of the Divine Love eliciting and enabling human response in love is to be found on almost every page of her written work. God as Love, enabling love in us, brings about our consummation in Love. Since this Love became incarnate in Jesus Christ, in his entire Paschal Mystery, our loving too has a "Christic" and paschal character that does not cease to be trinitarian at the same time. Letter 30 puts this vision beautifully and is worth quoting at some length:

> One finds oneself constrained by a gentle force to the constant practice of love, one receives the courage — henceforth happy and invincible — to face that state in which passion makes the Beloved grow in the being of the Loved One and to be penetrated by it in all things: to work with His hands, to walk with His feet, to hear with His ears where the divine voice never ceases to sound, to speak also through the mouth of the Beloved, in all truth, of counsel, of justice, of pure sweetness, of impartial consolation, of caution against evil — to appear like the Beloved without adornment of any kind, to live in nothing and for no one but in love and for the Beloved, to live like the Loved One with a single way of acting, a single thought, a single heart, to taste in him, as he in us, the inexpressible sweet-

ness that is the fruit of his sufferings — oh yes! To feel nothing but heart to heart, with a single heart, a single sweet love, to have fruition, one in the other, of the fullness of love — to know without any doubt, with an ever more perfect certainty, that one is integrated into the Unity of Love: in this way, one lives in the Father.[15]

This purple passage contains many good things. It is a fine example of the intertwining of Christian doctrines of which the First Vatican Council speaks: the Trinity is there; the deification or divinization of human beings through their engrafting into Love is there; the "Christification" of human beings is there. In a word, it is impossible to tap into any Christian doctrine without ineluctably finding oneself involved with the entire deposit of faith. This is how Hadewijch grasps doctrine: one doctrine leading to another, interpenetrating the other, and so forth.

For Hadewijch, then, God is the Trinity of the Christian tradition. Perhaps the finest expression of her trinitarian awareness comes in Letter 28, "Trinitarian Contemplation Caught in Words." In that letter there is a profound sense of God's gracious generosity, what Hadewijch refers to as "overflowingness":

A blessed soul saw with God according to God; and it saw God enclosed and yet overflowing. And it saw God overflowing in totality, and total in over-flowingness. And this soul spoke with its totality and exclaimed: "'God is a great and unique Lord in eternity, and he has in his Godhead the Being of Three Persons: He is Father in his power; he is Son in his knowableness; he is Holy Spirit in his glory. God gives, in the Father; and he reveals, in the Son; and he enables us to taste, in the Holy Spirit."[16]

God is supremely relational, "in his Godhead the Being of Three Persons," and in his "overflowingness" toward humankind, enabling us to taste the Godhead, as it were. With a sense of Hadewijch's doctrinal background, especially her trinitarian awareness, we are better placed to grasp something of her eucharistic thought.

Poem 16:30–45, in Hart's "Poems in Couplets," is entitled "Love's Seven Names" and includes some eucharistic reflections:

> (30) . . . And eats his flesh and drinks his blood:
> The heart of each devours the other's heart,
> One soul assaults the other and invades it completely,
> As who is Love itself showed us
> When he gave us himself to eat,
> (35) Disconcerting all the thoughts of man.
> By this he made known to us
> That love's most intimate union
> Is through eating, tasting, and seeing interiorly.
> He eats us; we think we eat him,
> (40) And we do eat him, of this we can be certain.
> But because he remains so undevoured,
> And so untouched, and so undesired,
> Each of us remains so uneaten by him
> And separated so far from each other.

Lines 31–35 suggest in very striking and powerful language the intimate and loving union between Christ and the soul, achieved through the Eucharist. "The heart of each devours the other's heart." The soul in love with Christ desires union with him, but that very desire for union is already anticipated by Christ in the institution of the Eucharist. At the foundational moment of the Last Supper, Christ provided the means by which union with him would be achieved. The God who is Love and loves us takes the initiative and is always ahead of us. His desire to be one with humankind is what is enabled and brought about through the Eucharist. And so, "love's most intimate union is through eating, tasting and seeing interiorly."

Hadewijch of Antwerp

The notion that Christ "eats us" may on first hearing sound strange. But is it so strange? Hadewijch had a great love of Augustine, as has been noted, and Hart states, "We are not surprised, therefore, to find in Hadewijch some specific instances of dependence upon him."[17] The intimacy of union focused on the Eucharist bringing about and expressing the whole Christ, head and members, is a commonplace of Augustinian theology. Think, for example, of the profound eucharistic theology and ecclesiology that comes to expression in Sermon 272, in which Augustine expresses his fascination for the dual meaning of the term "Body of Christ." It is both the people of God and the eucharistic gift, and the two meanings may not be separated: "The mystery that you are lies there on the table; it is your own mystery that you receive. . . . Be what you see, and receive what you are."[18] The two modes of Christ's Body are so ontologically connected that they are indissolubly one. One might also recall those remarkable words of Augustine from *The Confessions*, in a non-eucharistic context but certainly capable of a eucharistic interpretation:

> I found myself far from you "in the region of dissimilarity," and heard as it were your voice from on high: "I am the food of the fully grown; grow and you will feed on me. And you will not change me into you like the food your flesh eats, but you will be changed into me."[19]

For Hadewijch, Augustine's "You will be changed into me" comes about from Christ eating us, so to speak. The entire poem has a strong Augustinian feel to it, even if it is not possible to document that influence chapter and verse. At any rate, it is Hadewijch's version of a eucharistic ecclesiology. Notice how she points out the implications of not receiving the eucharistic Christ in lines 41–44. When Christ remains "undevoured and undesired," and so we are "uneaten by him," we are separated from the rest of the Body of Christ, the Church. The eucharistic Body of Christ makes the ecclesial Body of Christ. Not to participate in the former makes for separation and division in the latter.

The eucharistic reflections are found in Visions 1, 3, 4, 6, 7 and 12. Visions 1, 3 and 6 occurred after Hadewijch had received holy communion. In Vision 1:1 we read:

> It was a Sunday, in the Octave of Pentecost, when our Lord was brought secretly to my bedside, because I felt such an attraction of my spirit inwardly that I could not control myself outwardly in a degree sufficient to go among persons; it would have been impossible for me to go among them. And that desire which I had inwardly was to be one with God in fruition.

One wonders immediately why Hadewijch could not attend Mass and receive communion in that context, why it was impossible for her "to go among persons." In her commentary Hart suggests that Hadewijch is here describing the state of *orewoet*, a term that is difficult to translate but refers to a mystical state of "madness, or rage of love."[20] This mystical state likely had psychological and physical effects on her person that would have drawn not only attention to her, but also negative attention. After receiving communion in her own room, Hadewijch was drawn into deep eucharistic union with Christ: "When I had received our Lord, he then received me to him, so that he withdrew my senses from every remembrance of alien things to enable me to have joy in him in inward togetherness with him."[21] In the vision she recounts being led into a meadow planted with trees, and she provides an allegorical account of the various trees to which she is led. Gradually she is led to the "mighty place" where sat the One "whom I was seeking, and with whom I had desired to be one in fruition. . . . His eyes were marvelously unspeakable to see and drew all things to him in Love. . . . And my Beloved gave himself to me, both in spiritual understanding of himself and in feeling."[22] As the result of this experience of union with the Love that God is, she is given her mission: "My beloved, help all persons in their affliction impartially, whether they do you good or evil. Love will make you capable of it. Give all, for all is yours!"[23] The movement of the vision, consequent upon the reception of holy communion, appears to parallel the movement of the eucharistic celebration itself. After she arrives at some self-understanding and understanding of God, union with the Divine is achieved through God's gift of himself par excellence. That union has mission — being sent out —as its goal, so that by witness, commitment and service she may be an instrument of bringing others into the same union with Love.

Something similar happens in Vision 3:

> Later, one Easter Sunday, I had gone to God; and he embraced me in my interior senses and took me away in spirit. He brought me before the Countenance of the Holy Spirit, who possesses the Father and the Son in one Essence. . . . A voice issuing from this Countenance resounded so fearfully that it made itself heard above everything. And it said to me: ". . . With regard to all things, know what I, Love, am in them! And when you fully bring me yourself, as pure humanity in myself, through all the ways of perfect Love, you shall have fruition of me as the Love who I am. Until that day, you shall love what I, Love, am. And then you will be love, as I am Love. And you shall not live less than what I, Love, am, from that day until the death that will make you alive. In my unity, you have received me and I have received you. Go forth, and live what I am; and return bringing me full divinity, and have fruition of me as who I am."[24]

Again, one cannot help but notice the eucharistic sequence of the vision. On Easter Sunday, Hadewijch "had gone to God," that is, she received holy communion. From that eucharistic union, which, of course, lifts one up into the Trinity — she notes the Father, the Son and the Spirit in the vision — she is sent forth in mission, to act as Love's conduit of love, back to Love as the final term of the mission.

Vision 4 takes place at Mass during the reading of the Epistle
on the Feast of Saint James (Wisdom 5:1–5). As she listened to
the Epistle, "[Her] senses were drawn inwards with a great
tempestuous clamor by an awe-inspiring spirit that from within drew [her] within [herself]. From within [she] was then
wholly drawn into the spirit."[25] This should come as no surprise because that particular reading from the Book of
Wisdom speaks of God's witness as one "whom once we held
as a laughingstock and as a type for mockery. . . . His life we
accounted madness. . . . " Did Hadewijch recognize her own
difficult circumstances in this reading? It would have been
virtually impossible for her not to. Vision 6 takes place as she
experiences a great desire for holy communion: "Then it was
my will to go to our Lord; for at this time I experienced desires
and an exceedingly strong longing. . . . "[26] Vision 12 also comes
to her during Mass. The Mass, the one table of the Word and
the Eucharist, is the natural context, dare we say catalyst, for
Hadewijch's mystical visions.

Vision 7, however, which actually occurs during Matins, is the
climax of Hadewijch's "oneness in the Eucharist," to use
Hart's title for this vision. Hadewijch is beside herself with
desire for union with God: "The longing in which I then was
cannot be expressed by any language or any person I know. . . . I
can say this about it: I desired to have full fruition of my
Beloved, and to understand and taste him to the full."[27] This
full fruition with God is "to grow up in order to be God with
God." That which brings about this full fruition, being God
with God, is the Eucharist:

> Then he came from the altar, showing himself as a
> child. . . . He turned toward me, in his right hand
> took from the ciborium his body, and in his left
> hand took a chalice. . . . With that he came in the
> form and clothing of a Man, as he was on the day
> when he gave us his body for the first time. . . .
> Then he gave himself to me in the shape of the
> sacrament, in its outward form, as the custom is;

and then he gave me to drink from the chalice, in
form and taste, as the custom is. After that he came
himself to me, took me entirely in his arms, and
pressed me to him; and all my members felt his in
full felicity, in accordance with the desire of my
heart and my humanity.[28]

A number of things about this vision are particularly striking. First, the language is immediately suggestive of a docetic
christology in which Christ's humanity is only apparent and
not fully real — "showing himself as," "in the form and cloth-
ing of a Man." However, the fact that Hadewijch goes on to
speak of this Christ as first a child and then a mature man
demonstrates her sure grasp of his full humanity. The growth
of Christ from childhood to adulthood is her expression of
orthodox christology.

Second, when she says that "all [her] members felt his in full
felicity," she is saying that her full humanity is what reaches
union with God through the full but glorified humanity of
Christ. The entire movement of the incarnation through the
resurrection and ascension is not simply a past event for God,
but remains permanently and eternally in God. Christ's glorified humanity has not disappeared; if the full and real Christ
comes to her in holy communion, his glorified humanity is
part of that communing. Hadewijch would not have expressed
herself like this, but this comes close to her meaning. Thus,
eucharistic union with Christ is real and not notional.

Third, one cannot mistake the erotic nature of her language
in this vision. The celebrated medievalist Caroline Walker
Bynum remarks, "Hadewijch wrote both some of the most
affective, sensual, even erotic descriptions of union with
Christ ever penned. . . . "[29] If our modern sensibility is shocked
by this, it may be because a docetic perception of our own
humanity is at work in our spirituality. Being human means
all kinds of things, but it includes being sexual. If sexuality is
part of God's good creation, why should we be surprised that

an intelligent and passionate woman like Hadewijch uses erotic language in the attempt to convey what she cannot adequately describe otherwise, that is, union with the incomprehensible God? However, it is important to note the sequence. She does not set out to provide a clinical, analytical account of mystical union with God. Rather, she *experiences* through God's grace such union and subsequently casts around for language that will convey something of this to others: erotic language clearly has the capacity for expressing profound intimacy. This erotic language is not peculiar to Hadewijch but is shared by many mystics.

Nonetheless, it is arguable that with the Reformation (reinforced subsequently during and after the Enlightenment) came a tendency for European culture and theology to hold in suspicion aspects and expressions of mysticism that involved the fleshly and the bodily. The Anglican ecclesiastical historian, Sister Benedicta Ward, S.L.G., sagely points out: "There was a new stress on what was intellectually orthodox. . . . In a united Europe, where Christian teaching was mostly clearly articulated and heretics were few, visionaries had been easily accepted and indeed cherished, their orthodoxy unquestioned. In the sixteenth century under the pressure of heresy, the evidence of the experiences of the ecstatic visionaries was received with a new caution."[30] Fuelled by the subsequent Enlightenment, modern people sometimes feel uncomfortable with the accounts and the language, including erotic language, of mystical experiences of earlier ages.

Perhaps also the Enlightenment's predilection for knowing as conceptual and analytical precluded what might be called "bodily knowing," which is neither less real nor less genuine. Hadewijch's language of eucharistic union is an expression of bodily knowing; it is affective, rooted in feeling and emotion. One theologian summarizes bodily knowing in these terms: "Not only by reason, but also in and through their bodies do human beings know other human beings in their humanness, their personalness. Not only by reason but also in and through their bodies do human beings know much that is intrinsically precious in human life. The recognition of this fact does away with any medieval or modern epistemology that propounds a hierarchy of knowledge."[31] If the rational and analytical approach to knowledge that marks our *modern* world is the child of the Enlightenment, then perhaps as we now see some of the more problematic aspects of the Enlightenment, we are discovering what might be called *post-modern* ways of knowing. In this sense, it may not be wrong to think of Hadewijch as a post-modern thinker.

The Eucharist, then, is central to Hadewijch's mystical experience. The Eucharist for her is the primary mechanism by which Love transforms us, and we become Love. That transformation by Love implies a constant performance of love in human lives until that day when we come alive in death. Here in Hadewijch is an *experiential* eucharistic ecclesiology, an understanding that the Eucharist makes the Church, that the Body of Christ makes the Body of Christ, not abstractly in some neat theological system, but in the living experience of what it means to be fed with Christ.

Conclusion

If Hildegard of Bingen was a woman writing monastic theology, Hadewijch of Antwerp was a woman writing vernacular theology. Bernard McGinn of the University of Chicago maintains that for a balanced sense of the Middle Ages, one must recognize that there were three forms of medieval theology: the scholastic, the monastic and the vernacular. What he means by vernacular theology is a theology written in the developing vernacular languages of medieval Europe.[32] This is exactly what Hadewijch had done, written theology in her own language and not in the ecclesiastical Latin of the period, written theology out of her own mystical experience of the Divine Love and not in the terms of scholasticism. She also offers to the laity of today the example of one given over to the worship, praise and union with Love, especially through the Eucharist, as one of themselves. Hadewijch of Antwerp invites us to become more, much more than we are.

Hadewijch of Antwerp

1   "The Beguines," in John A. Nichols and Lillian T. Shank, ed., *Distant Echoes: Medieval Religious Women*, Kalamazoo MI: Cistercian Publications, 1984, p. 184. See also David L. Edwards, *Christianity: The First Two Thousand Years*, Maryknoll NY: Orbis Books, 1997, pp. 226–27.

2   Caroline Walker Bynum, *Holy Feast and Holy Fast: The Religious Significance of Food to Medieval Women*, Berkeley-Los Angeles-London: University of California Press, 1987, p. 153.

3   Emily Zum Brunn and Georgette Epiney-Burgard, *Women Mystics in Medieval Europe*, (tr. S. Hughes), New York: Paragon House, 1989, p. 97.

4   Ibid., p. 98.

5   Vision 1:185, *Hadewijch, The Complete Works*, Translation and Introduction by Mother Columba Hart, O.S.B., Preface by Paul Mommaers, New York-Ramsey-Toronto: Paulist Press, 1980, p. 266.

6   Vision 4:44, ibid., p. 273.

7   Letter 25, ibid., pp. 105–06.

8   Ibid., p. 4.

9   Ibid., p. 5.

10   Vision 11:49, ibid., p. 290.

11   Zum Brunn and Epiney-Burgard, op. cit., p. 98. Louis Bouyer writes, "We have, in the person of Hadewijch, a spiritual master almost without equal as well as an exquisite feminine figure, endowed with the greatest gifts of intelligence and of heart as well as culture" *(Women Mystics*, [tr. A. E. Nash], San Francisco: Ignatius Press, 1993, p. 17). See also the comments on Hadewijch in Jean Leclercq, Francois Vandenbroucke and Louis Bouyer, *The Spirituality of the Middle Ages*, London: Burns and Oates, 1968, pp. 361–64.

12   Hart, *Hadewijch*, op. cit.

13   Op. cit., p. 191.

14   Bouyer, *Women Mystics*, p. 23.

15   Barbara Newman, *From Virile Woman to WomanChrist*, Philadelphia: University of Pennsylvania Press, 1995, pp. 157–58.

16   Letter 28:101, *Hadewijch: The Complete Works*, pp. 110–11.

17   Ibid., p. 6.

18   Augustine, *Sermon 272*. See William Harmless, *Augustine and the Catechumenate*, Collegeville: The Liturgical Press, 1995, pp. 316–24.

19   *Confessions*, 7:10:16, (tr. Henry Chadwick), Oxford and New York: Oxford University Press, 1991, pp. 123–24.

2   Zum Brunn and Epiney-Burgard, op. cit., p. 100.

21   Vision 1:15, *Hadewijch: The Complete Works*, p. 263.

22   Vision 1:246, ibid., p. 267.

23   Vision 1:408, ibid., p. 271.

24   Ibid., p. 272.

25   Ibid., p. 273.

26   Ibid., p. 278.

27   Vision 7:14, ibid., p. 280.

28   Vision 7:57–64, ibid., p. 281.

29   Op. cit., pp. 153–54.

30   Benedicta Ward, S.L.G., "Saints and Sybils: Hildegard of Bingen to Teresa of Avila," in Janet Martin Soskice, ed., *After Eve: Women, Theology and the Christian Tradition*, London: Collins-Marshall Pickering, 1990, p. 111.

31   John Giles Milhaven, *Hadewijch and Her Sisters: Other Ways of Loving and Knowing*, Albany NY: State University of New York Press, 1993, p. 119. See also Grace M. Jantzen, *Power, Gender and Christian Mysticism*, Cambridge University Press, 1995, pp. 135–37, 145–46.

32   Bernard McGinn, "Introduction," in Bernard McGinn, ed., *Meister Eckhart and the Beguine Mystics*, New York: The Continuum Publishing Company, 1994, pp. 1–14.

Chapter 3

Beatrice of Nazareth

The medieval mystic and Cistercian nun Beatrice of Nazareth is not well known outside the Netherlands and Belgium — indeed, Bernard McGinn says, "Only recently has [she] begun to take her rightful place among the major women mystics of the later Middle Ages."[1] However, like her contemporary Hadewijch of Antwerp, Beatrice's theological reflections are of interest not only from the point of view of the history and theological literature of her period, but also for their relevance in our own spiritual and eucharistic lives. One specialist in medieval mysticism indicates the importance of Beatrice's contribution when she writes, "Beatrice, along with Hadewijch . . . stands at the fountainhead of Flemish vernacular spirituality and forms a link between the Latin theological literature produced by Bernard of Clairvaux, William of St. Thierry, Aelred of Rievaulx, Richard of St. Victor and the later vernacular writers and mystics, Ruysbroeck and Meister Eckhart."[2] The fact that Beatrice has been so little known is now changing because of her unintended but real bridge building between Latin and her native Flemish and because of the considerable research that has been conducted in recent years.

Beatrice was born about 1200 in Tienen, a town not far from Brussels and about twenty kilometers east of Louvain.[3] Her pious and devout parents belonged to the well-to-do middle class and were perhaps involved in the lucrative textile trade of Flanders.[4] She appears to have been the youngest of six children and, according to the tradition, she was able to recite the psalms by heart at five years of age, having been taught how to read by her mother, Gertrude. After her mother's death when Beatrice was about seven, her father, Bartholomew, placed her with the community of Beguines at Zoutleauw.[5]

While she lived in the Beguine community, her academic formation went ahead under teachers in the same town. Later, her father transferred her to the Cistercian Abbey of Bloemendaal, for which he was acting as financial manager, and she continued her education there. When she was about sixteen, Beatrice was received into religious life at Bloemendaal; two of her sisters, Christine and Sybille, also joined the community about this time.

After Beatrice's religious profession at Bloemendaal, the abbess sent her to the Cistercian community of Rameya to learn how to transcribe and illuminate manuscripts. During her time at Rameya, from 1216 to 1217, she became an intimate friend of Ida of Nivelles (1199–1231), who was known and respected for her understanding of spiritual matters. That both had spent time with the Beguines would have afforded an immediate common bond between them.[6] With Ida's care and guidance there can be no doubt that Beatrice advanced in the spiritual life. Her father, Bartholomew, and her brother, Wickbert, also joined the community at Bloemendaal as lay-brothers; when the community established a foundation at Maagdendaal, which was close to their hometown of Tienen, Bartholomew and his children were sent there. This, however, was not to be the end of Beatrice's monastic translation. In 1235 another foundation was made at Nazareth, near Lier. In 1236 Beatrice, Christine and Sybille were transferred to that foundation, hence the name Beatrice of Nazareth. The following year she became prioress and remained in that office until her death in 1268.

From an early age, Beatrice had kept notes on her ascetic and mystical experiences. While these notes have not themselves survived — Bernard McGinn describes them as "a lost mystical journal" — after her death they were edited and translated into Latin by a Cistercian monk, probably a confessor at the Abbey of Nazareth, in the form of a biography.[7] This text, known as "The Life of Beatrice," is made up of a prologue and three books; each book corresponds to the three stages of the spiritual life: beginner, proficient, perfect. From data in this biography, a treatise entitled "On Divine Love and Its Seven Steps" has been recognized as the personal work of Beatrice. This treatise has been identified with "The Seven Manners of Loving," the oldest extant text in Flemish;[8] it deals with the ascent of the soul to God in a fashion reminiscent of Saint Teresa of Avila's seven castles of the soul, and is "perhaps the first text written by a woman that can be described as essentially mystagogical, that is, designed to guide others along the path of interior transformation toward direct contact with God."[9]

The Seven Manners of Loving

As Beatrice puts it, Love (in Flemish *Minne*) is the process of maturation of the soul with God, and it is marked by Seven Manners "which come down from the highest place and which return again to the summit from which they came."[10] Love/*Minne* "signifies the fundamental reality or power by which all things participate in God and by which they return to him."[11] The entire process is grace-filled, beginning with God and returning to God.

The First Manner of Loving is "a great and fervent longing to arrive at that liberty, purity, and nobility of spirit in which she had been created according to the image and likeness of the Creator."[12] It is the basic choice of aspiring to union with God, the very choice and aspiration, however, having been placed there by God. Consequent upon this basic choice is the need to remove obstacles that stand in the way of this union, "putting to flight her defects."[13] One commentator aptly describes this First Manner "as an apprenticeship," since the tools of the trade are being learned and the skills developed to enable that desired union with God to occur.[14]

The Second Manner of Loving "sets itself the task to serve our Lord freely out of love alone, without any other motive and without any reward of grace or glory."[15] This stage is described as "beyond measure, beyond human sense and reason." It is described in this fashion because in the light of authentic self-knowledge there can be no rational *apologia* for this total self-gift. To love so totally, expecting nothing in return, is beyond comprehension.

The dominant characteristic of the Third Manner is pain and suffering. The soul, desiring to serve God so totally and completely, in every possible respect, with all excellence, finds itself painfully frustrated by its sheer inability. "Its greatest sorrow is that it cannot satisfy love according to its own greatest desire. . . . It knows well that such fulfillment surpasses all human capacity and all her own strength. . . . What it ought to desire but cannot attain is a great pain to it."[16]

The Fourth and Fifth Manners may be compared to the two panels of a diptych.[17] This is how Beatrice describes them: "Our Lord is also accustomed to give other manners of loving, at one time with great pleasure, but at another with great sorrow."[18] The first panel of the diptych is sweetness, in which God consoles the soul:

> And then the heart is so touched with tender love,
> is drawn towards love with such desire, is
> embraced so cordially by love, is subjected by love
> so strongly, and is held in love's embrace so loving-
> ly, that it is wholly conquered by love. In this the
> heart feels a great closeness to God.[19]

The other panel of the diptych reverts to the pain and suffering of the Third Manner, in which the soul experiences its utter inability to satisfy its desire to love God gratuitously: "The soul experiences suffering without any cause from the great sense of love, or it may be from what it has specially requested by its longing for love, or because it suffers from having no fruition of love."[20]

The Sixth Manner emerges when all the heart-rending tensions and contradictions of the Fifth Manner are eliminated:

"The soul feels that love has conquered all her adversaries within her, has corrected her defects and subdued her senses, has adorned her nature, has amplified and exalted her state of soul and gained dominion over herself without contradiction that she . . . can delight in it in peace."[21] In the Seventh Manner the soul is drawn "through eternal Love alone into the eternity of Love, and into the incomprehensibility and vastness and inaccessible sublimity and deep abyss of the godhead."[22] Union with God is now complete.

When inquiring into Beatrice's eucharistic spirituality in the Seven Manners, nothing explicit is to be found. Her eucharistic reflections and appreciation emerge in *The Life of Beatrice,* but in the context of the Seven Manners of Love. The Seven Manners of Love provide the mystical map for final union with the God who is Love, but the Eucharist is the food that enables one to follow the map, as it were.

The Eucharist

Most of the theologians of the eleventh and twelfth centuries wrote about the Eucharist. In fact, one student of this period reckons that over 150 treatises on the Eucharist have been identified.[23] Debates and variant points of view, especially concerning the eucharistic presence, flourished and prepared the backdrop for the Fourth Lateran Council in 1215. That council said of the Eucharist: "Jesus Christ is both priest and sacrifice, whose body and blood are truly contained in the sacrament of the altar under the species of bread and wine; the bread having by the power of God been transubstantiated into the body and the wine into the blood, whereby we receive of his what he received of ours so that the mystery of unity may be perfected."[24] Two elements of this teaching are of particular importance, both to understand Beatrice and to learn from her: the real eucharistic presence of Christ "truly contained in the sacrament of the altar," and the purpose of that presence, our divinization — "we receive of his what he received of ours so that the mystery of unity may be perfected." Roger De Ganck describes the holy women of this century such as Ida of

Louvain, Hadewijch of Antwerp and Beatrice of Nazareth as not only accepting this teaching as the teaching of the Church, but as having "a passion for it."[25] This is a fine description of Beatrice's appreciation of the Eucharist and of the challenge that she offers the contemporary Church.

The Eucharist is for her a medicine. She resists the temptation of the devil to "shake from her heart through torpor and cowardice the healthy desire for this life-giving sacrament received from the Lord," and receives the sacrament regularly so as not to be deprived of "this medicinal support."[26] Thus, the Eucharist is "the health-giving sacrament of his body and blood, which he left to the human race both as a reminder of himself and as its support and traveling provision in this wandering exile."[27] The word for "traveling provision" here is the beautiful eucharistic word *viaticum*, still very much in use in our tradition.

Viewing the Eucharist as medicinal has a long history in the tradition of eucharistic reflection, going back to Ignatius of Antioch who in the early second century describes the Eucharist as "the medicine of immortality."[28] Mortality is understood as a wound or a disease healed by the Eucharist that enables our sharing in the immortality proper to God. That the Eucharist is our healing and our immortality is an aspect of eucharistic thinking quite alien to many today. While the issue is admittedly complex, one of the reasons for contemporary failure to receive this dimension of the Eucharist has to do with increasing awareness of the healing properties and benefits of modern medicine and technology. Surgical procedures, technological apparatus and pharmacology are the founts of healing for us, and so they should be; but this healing of which Beatrice and the tradition speaks is not the immediate healing that comes from medical professionals. This healing quite simply recognizes that just as our origin lies in God, so too does our final end, our final healing. At the center of our human lives, as their staff and stay, is the Eucharist, sacramentally anticipating the healing we finally desire, even as we are less than conscious of it.

Beatrice of Nazareth

Recently I rediscovered something of this magnificent eucharistic insight in reading the book *Encounter with Mystery*, which describes the L'Arche communities founded by Jean Vanier.[29] Vanier and his colleagues look after people who are suffering from mental handicaps. In terms of immediate healing, modern medicine can do almost nothing for such people, but in these vibrant communities of love the mentally handicapped are prepared for and receive the Eucharist. *Encounter with Mystery* offers the stories of some for whom medicine holds no hope but who find what can be called healing only in the Eucharist. A priest and chaplain in one of the L'Arche communities writes, "The Eucharist is the height of the experience whereby the presence of Jesus is made known through people with mental handicaps and through their assistants." He goes on to provide the example of Laurent, a profoundly handicapped young man who had been in a psychiatric institution since he was three years old: "It can be quite surprising to hear the reflections of all those assistants who have taken friends such as Laurent to Mass. They are unanimous in saying that they experience the Mass in a new way, discovering a new intensity of Jesus' presence, and receiving a gift of compassion leading to a new depth of communion."[30] Laurent experiences healing, closeness to God, in his utterly childlike reception of holy communion, but so do his caregivers as they observe him. Maybe it is only when the normal apparatus of medicine fails, that we are graced with a sense of the healing that the Eucharist brings, a healing as *viaticum* not only for the end, but on the way.

In a similar vein, Beatrice refers to the Eucharist as "the deifying sacrament."[31] These descriptions of the Eucharist are, of course, dependent upon the strong, realistic sense of Christ's presence. This presence is effected through the power of the Holy Spirit in the eucharistic prayer, at the center of which is the consecration, and so the elevation of the consecrated host is particularly precious to Beatrice. "At the elevation of the deifying sacrament Beatrice saw a ray of incomprehensible clarity flashing like lightning from the Lord's sacred body; it penetrated her inmost heart with its flaming brightness and drew her spirit wholly to itself."[32] Sometimes the elevation of the host is interpreted pejoratively as a medieval substitute for actually receiving holy communion; there is some truth in this, but not for Beatrice. So profound is her grasp of Christ's presence in the celebration of Mass that she can hardly wait for communion: "[Christ] was so strongly attracting her with the bond of that love which surpasses all human understanding that she could scarcely wait for the usual time for Communion, but with open heart and with enlarged veins, as if she were mad with excessive desire, she aspired in a certain wondrous gesture to receive the Lord's saving body."[33] Her vision of the elevated host propels her towards communion. Receiving the sacrament for Beatrice is no social convention, but rather Christ's divine advent and the herald and agent of our advent into divinity.

As one might expect, a profound awareness of receiving the sacramental Christ in this fashion had behavioral consequences. Some of these consequences for Beatrice took the form of extreme asceticism. This is how one scholar summarizes the portrayal of Beatrice in the autobiography: "This autobiography makes it clear that Beatrice tortured her body in extreme asceticism — flagellating herself, sleeping on stones, walking on ice, binding thorns between her breasts and around her loins, and, even in illness, eating only dry bread — and that devotion to the Eucharist was at the heart of her piety."[34] Needless to say, such practices are strange to us and, indeed, seem to depreciate the body, especially in its sexual aspect. No one would wish to endorse such practices today, but is it possible for us to see also something positive at work in this extreme asceticism? Take, for example, Beatrice's reluctance to eat ordinary food. "Like the mad and insane she would apply her sense and mind only under external coercion or rebuke to what is recognized as useful to sustaining the body."[35] Granting the ascetic excess here, nevertheless one can see in her reaction the overwhelming recognition of Christ's presence and the perduring invitation to commune with this

Christ without things getting in the way. As Roger De Ganck puts it, "The psychosomatic phenomena and other circumstances related to the Eucharist should not distract us from the basic and essential element: the encounter with Christ himself."[36] It is certainly arguable that our modern age has lost something of this conviction that Christ is really, sacramentally present in the Eucharist, and that such practices as brief and limited fasting before and after holy communion may contribute to a salutary retrieval of this aspect of the faith. If no boundaries are in place between us and the Eucharist, between our daily routines and the sacredness of Christ's presence, we lose a sense of that sacredness.

Conclusion

We cannot enter the age of Beatrice; our culture and our times are quite different, and aspects of her asceticism are repugnant to us. Theology, however, involves the ability to listen across the centuries for the accent of truth and, having found it, to blend that accent with our own speech. As we listen with care to the accent of truth found in Beatrice, we can re-sonate, re-sound, with her sense of phased union with God, brought about primarily through the Eucharist. The healing Eucharist, a burning desire to be in communion with the eucharistic Christ — these truths for which Beatrice stands are part of the Church's treasury of eucharistic reflection. The eucharistic Christ told us, "Every scribe who has been trained for the kingdom of heaven is like a householder who brings out of his treasure what is new and what is old"(Matthew 13:52). The newly re-discovered Beatrice of Nazareth offers us from the thirteenth century not a heroine for slavish imitation, but the riches of eucharistic conviction no less necessary in our day than in hers.

[1] Bernard McGinn, *The Flowering of Mysticism: Men and Women in the New Mysticism 1200–1350*, New York: The Crossroad Publishing Company, 1998, p. 173.

[2] Mary Anne Sullivan, O.C.S.O., "An Introduction to the *Vita Beatricis*," in John A. Nichols and Lillian T. Shank, O.C.S.O., ed., *Hidden Springs: Cistercian Monastic Women*, Kalamazoo: Cistercian Publications Inc., 1995, p. 355.

[3] For the biographical information I am much indebted to Roger De Ganck, "Beatrice's Curriculum Vitae," in *The Life of Beatrice of Nazareth, 1200–1268*, translated and annotated by Roger De Ganck, assisted by John Baptist Hasbrouck, O.C.S.O., Kalamazoo MI: Cistercian Publications, Inc., 1991, pp. xiii–xix.

Beatrice of Nazareth

4 Sullivan, op. cit., p. 347.

5 For basic information about the Beguines, see pp. 21–23 above.

6 Martinus Cawley, O.C.S.O., "Ida of Nivelles: Cistercian Nun," in Nichols and Shank, op. cit., p. 307. Cawley has recently translated into English Goswin de Bossut, *Life of Ida the Compassionate of Nivelles,* Lafayette OR: Guadalupe Translations, 1998.

7 McGinn, op. cit., p. 167.

8 See Ritamary Bradley, O.C.S.O., "Love and Knowledge in *Seven Manners of Loving,*" in Nichols and Shank, op. cit., pp. 361–76.

9 McGinn, op. cit., p. 168.

10 De Ganck, *The Life of Beatrice of Nazareth,* op. cit., p. 289.

11 Bernard McGinn, op. cit., p. 171.

12 De Ganck, *The Life of Beatrice of Nazareth,* op. cit., p. 291.

13 Ibid., p. 293.

14 Emilie Zum Brunn and Georgette Epiney-Burgard, *Women Mystics in Medieval Europe,* (tr. S. Hughes), New York: Paragon House, 1989, p. 81.

15 De Ganck, *The Life of Beatrice of Nazareth,* op. cit., p. 295.

16 Ibid., pp. 300–01.

17 This helpful comparison comes from Zum Brunn and Epiney-Burgard, op. cit., p. 81.

18 De Ganck, *The Life of Beatrice of Nazareth,* op. cit., p. 303.

19 Ibid., pp. 304–05.

20 Ibid., p. 309.

21 Ibid., p. 319.

22 Ibid., p. 321.

23 Gary Macy, *The Banquet's Wisdom: A Short History of the Theologies of the Lord's Supper,* New York and Mahwah: Paulist Press, 1992, p. 85.

24 Joseph Neuner and Jacques Dupuis, ed., *The Christian Faith,* London: Collins, 1983, p. 203.

25 Roger De Ganck, *Beatrice of Nazareth in Her Context,* Kalamazoo MI: Cistercian Publications, 1991, p. 309.

26 De Ganck, *The Life of Beatrice of Nazareth,* op. cit., p. 181.

27 Ibid., pp. 122–23.

28 Ignatius of Antioch, *Letter to the Ephesians,* 20:2.

29 Frances M. Young, ed., *Encounter with Mystery: Reflections on L'Arche and Living with Disability,* London: Darton, Longman and Todd, 1997.

30 Ibid., pp. 35–37.

31 Ibid., pp. 103, 181, 279.

32 Ibid., p. 279.

33 Ibid., p. 225.

34 Caroline Walker Bynum, *Holy Feast and Holy Fast: The Religious Significance of Food to Medieval Women,* Berkeley-Los Angeles-London: University of California Press, 1987, p. 161.

35 De Ganck, *The Life of Beatrice of Nazareth,* op. cit., p. 189.

36 De Ganck, *Beatrice of Nazareth in Her Context,* p. 335.

Chapter 4

Mechthild of Magdeburg

Mechthild was born between 1207 and 1210 in the diocese of Magdeburg. Apparently well educated, she began to have mystical experiences when she was about twelve. About 1230 Mechthild left her family to enter a Beguine community in the city of Magdeburg. She did not reveal her spiritual experiences to anyone but her confessor, Henry of Halle, who encouraged her to write about them. In 1250, writing in German, she began *The Flowing Light of the Godhead*, which Henry later edited and translated into Latin.[1] The entire text runs to seven books: The first six were compiled by Henry and, after his death, the seventh was completed at the Helfta convent where Mechthild spent her old age. The text consists largely of a series of poems interspersed with prose; it was intended to be used by Christians generally, not just by the Beguine community.[2] Mechthild was aware that her book was not well received by everyone, partly because of her intensely human imagery for the relationship of the soul with God: "I was warned against writing this book. People said: 'If one did not watch out, it could be burned. . . .'" But God reassured her: "My dear one, do not be overly troubled. No one can burn the truth. For someone to take this book out of my hand, he must be mightier than I. The book is threefold and portrays me alone."[3] Commenting on the strength of this statement, and similar statements by women mystics in the thirteenth century, Bernard McGinn writes: "To the best of my knowledge, no medieval male mystics ever made quite the same claims for the divine authorization of their texts that we see advanced by the female evangelists of the thirteenth century."[4]

The possibility of the book's being burned did not arise only from the daring expression of her teaching. Mechthild castigated the clergy of her times for what she regarded as corruption; needless to say, this made enemies for her and increased the opposition that she experienced. Thus, in her old age she left Magdeburg for the Cistercian convent at Helfta, where she was received in 1270 by the Abbess Gertrude of Hackeborn. Hans Urs von Balthasar describes Mechthild's reception: "The cultured and refined women of Helfta welcomed the elderly weather-beaten sibyl with veneration and awe."[5]

As she was writing the last part of her book in the convent at Helfta, Mechthild clearly felt that the energy and the forces that nourished her earlier in life were simply no longer present. This is how she expresses herself: "Seven years ago a discouraged old person complained to God about this sorry state of things. God gave this reply: 'Your childhood was a playmate of my Holy Spirit. Your youth was a bride of my humanity. Your old age is now a housewife of my Godhead.'"[6] It was true that she did not have the energy and gifts of earlier years, but now she had reached the stage of being a "housewife of God." Her decline in life was unquestionable, but to be a house-wife/*Hausfrau* of the Godhead was no mean grace. The grace would reach its final completion when the soul went to God: "Thus does [the soul] speak: 'The long waiting is coming to an end.' In the future God and the soul shall be united, unseparated forever. Whenever I think about it, my heart feels intense joy."[7]

Mechthild's preferred literary genre is the dialogue or conversation — with God, with her own soul, with the angels. In these dialogues she "had little or no use for the theoretical; her own experience of God was the starting point and impetus of all her writings."[8]

Aspects of Mechthild's Theology

The Trinity is central for Mechthild, the Trinity that "flows." "Flowing" is a key word for her understanding of God, a flowing *within* the Trinity and a flowing *from* the Trinity in creation and redemption, a flowing that also returns the soul to God:

> I shall greet the sublimity, the splendor, the bliss,
> the wisdom, the nobility and the wondrous oneness

of the Holy Trinity. Out of it has flowed forth immaculate all that was, that is, that ever shall be. There I must one day enter again. . . .[9]

When she speaks of "one day enter[ing] again" into the Trinity, she is not in the strict sense speaking of some pre-existence of souls in God so much as the notion that the entirety of God's flowing in creation is immediately present to God, including the individual soul.

It is, however, not the immanent Trinity of scholastic speculation that is her concern, but the Trinity imaged from her own experience. In a reflection that has to do with a self-willed member of her community "who causes [her] much distress because of her contrary disposition," whose selfish will has given the devil power, Mechthild finds consolation in the Trinity: "My soul flew to God so swiftly that she literally arose with no effort on her part and snuggled herself into the Holy Trinity, just as a child snuggles into its mother's coat and lays itself right at her breast."[10] It is a lovely image whose loveliness is rooted in the sheer ordinariness of womanly and maternal experience. The soul wanted the comfort of her maternal God and found it with ease.

Another trinitarian image emerges from the experience of drinking wine. She images heaven as a house:

> The heavenly Father is the blessed chalice-bearer there and Jesus the chalice, the Holy Spirit the unadulterated wine . . . the whole Trinity is the full chalice and Love the mistress in charge of the wine cellar, then, God knows, I will be happy indeed if love invites me into the house.[11]

A number of themes are inextricably entangled here. Wine, of course, immediately suggests the Eucharist; after the Last Supper, Jesus had asked in the garden of Gethsemane that the chalice of suffering would pass from him (Luke 22:42). At the same time, "the whole Trinity is the full chalice," and so without severe theological analysis Mechthild has articulated a trinitarian sense of the Eucharist. Her experience of drinking wine and her experience of the Eucharist inter-flow and inter-penetrate to produce a healthy kind of incarnational, experiential theology.

In *The Flowing Light,* 3:9, God's plan of creation and redemption is described as a conversation among the persons of the Trinity: the Spirit and the Son speaking with the Father about sharing existence with others — Adam and Eve — and then redeeming that existence after the Fall. It is the standard schema of creation and redemption, yet here again Mechthild finds her experience of life yielding insight into the divine mystery. The Holy Spirit becomes a musician, most probably a harpist, playing for the Father:

> Then the Holy Spirit in his superabundance played for the Father, plucking the Holy Trinity, and said to him: "Lord, dear Father, I shall give you out of yourself generous advice. We no longer wish to go on thus, not bearing fruit. We shall have a created kingdom and you shall form the angels in my image so that they are one spirit with me. . . ." The Father said: "You are one spirit with me. What you suggest and want is to my liking."[12]

The harp the Holy Spirit is playing is the Trinity, "plucking the Holy Trinity," and the Father and the Spirit are "one spirit" or, as we say in the Nicene Creed, "one in being." There is clear orthodoxy in her doctrine, but its expression is experiential. The judgment of Edith Scholl is surely on target: "Obviously, this is far from the language of scholastic theology. Yet how vivid and real it makes the Three persons in their individuality and unity!"[13]

Mechthild's experiential approach to the Trinity is undoubtedly orthodox, but her orthodoxy has something of a daring

Mechthild of Magdeburg

character about it. *The Flowing Light of the Godhead* contains some erotic passages, what might be described as a "spiritual sexuality," as she seeks to find ways not only of speaking her desire for God, but also God's desire for her and for every human soul. In fact, Bernard McGinn says of this aspect of Mechthild's thought: "Mechthild's mastery of the language of love marks her out as one of the premier voices in the history of erotic mysticism in Christianity."[14] Thus we come across this passage, with God as the speaker:

> I cannot be completely intimate with her [the soul] unless she is willing to lay herself in utter repose and nakedness in my divine arms, so that I can take delight in her. For it was for this that I surrendered myself into her power — like a child, poor, naked, bare, scorned, and finally into death — that she alone — ah, if she desires it — might be my closest, my dearest companion. And she shall ever more in soul and body soar about and play to her heart's content in my Holy Trinity and drink herself full like the fish in the sea.[15]

The strength of what God has to say about his unitive intimacy with the soul, "completely intimate with her . . . repose and nakedness," is softened by the change of metaphor, "like a child. . . ." It is almost as if Mechthild, realizing her audacious mode of expression, tones it down with the more conventionally acceptable references to the child. However, like her Beguine sisters Hadewijch and Beatrice who also use erotic images, the strength of the imagery should be allowed to stand. One of the most powerful of human experiences is sexual union. The Church uses this image of union to speak of the indissoluble link between the Church and Christ, for example in 1 Corinthians 5:15ff., or Ephesians 5:25ff. Mechthild is but taking this line of imagery a stage further and personalizing it, as it were. She sees God, the Trinity, as the ultimate, passionate, restless lover burning with desire for his creatures.[16]

Nor does Mechthild lack a sense of the Church and, indeed, of her responsibility for the Church. She has "three children that [she] see[s] suffering great distress . . . poor sinners which lie in eternal death . . . the poor souls who are tormented in purgatory . . . the imperfect in religious life."[17] The Church suffering in purgatory, the Church suffering from sin and lukewarmness — all are her concern.

Eucharist

Mechthild has a profound sense of her unworthiness to attend Mass and to receive the Eucharist. In a vision of the Eucharist unfolding, she sees the church filling with all the ecclesial ranks — saints, apostles, martyrs, angels, blessed souls. Perhaps because of her medieval sense of social order allied to her sense of unworthiness to receive the sacrament, she is not quite sure where to position herself. And so she reflects, "Did she dare stay there in her wretched condition?"[18] This sense of unworthiness, however, does not prevent her going to communion: "[S]hall I, the least of souls, take [Jesus Christ] in my arms, eat him and drink him, and have my way with him." As the passage continues, she recognizes that not even the angels have this unique eucharistic privilege:

> This can never happen to the angels. No matter how high he dwells above me, his Godhead shall never be so distant that I cannot constantly entwine my limbs with him; and so I shall never cool off. What, then, do I care what the angels experience?[19]

At the same time, she realizes that serious sin puts one at a distance from receiving holy communion: "If a person did not confess a sin and has no intention of confessing it, he should not receive God's body."[20]

On one occasion she experienced an apparition of the devil, trying to tempt her from the straight path. The devil looked like Christ, with "the five wounds painted on his feet and hands," but Mechthild said to him: "You are telling me that you are God. Well then, tell me, who is that who is the Son of the living God, now here in the true priest's hands?"[21] She demonstrates here a firm belief in the eucharistic presence of Christ. This sense of the eucharistic presence is a fully trinitarian sense for Mechthild:

> In these words I saw in the Holy Trinity this explanation: Whenever we receive God's Body, the Godhead unites itself to our innocent soul and God's humanity mixes itself with our hideous body, and thus does the Holy Spirit make his dwelling in our faith.[22]

The clear awareness of the Trinity noted above permeates her entire understanding of spiritual matters.

Eating and drinking God by no means provides a guarantee of spiritual bliss for Mechthild. Suffering is part of the Christian life and ought not to be shunned. This comes to expression in a eucharistic vision focusing on the blood of Christ. She had a vision of Christ:

> In his hands [appeared] two golden chalices that were both full of living wine. In his left hand was the red wine of suffering, and in his right hand the white wine of sublime consolation. Then our Lord spoke: "Blessed are those who drink this red wine. Although I give both out of divine love, the white wine is nobler in itself; but noblest of all are those who drink both the white and the red."[23]

A vision of the Eucharist being celebrated by Saint John the Baptist appears in Book 6; this vision caused her trouble because the Baptist was not a priest but a layman, who could not preside at the Eucharist. Here is her reflection:

My Pharisee remarked in response . . . that John
the Baptist was a layman. The Most Holy
Sacrament in the Mass is God's body. John the
Baptist touched this same Son of God in humble
trembling fear while leading a holy life of such dig-
nity that he heard the voice of the heavenly Father
and caught his words and saw the Holy Spirit and
recognized the Son in them both. John the Baptist
also preached the holy Christian faith openly to all
the people and pointed out for the people with his
finger the true Son of God who was there present:
"Behold the Lamb of God."[24]

Her thinking is fascinating! John the Baptist touched the really present Christ at the moment of his baptism, but, of course,
only priests touch the sacred body of Christ, the real presence
of Christ; and John also proclaimed to the people, "Behold the
Lamb of God," the words the priest proclaims in the communion rite. Thus Mechthild finishes this passage with a
flourish of rhetorical victory: "Was this man really a layman?
Prove me wrong, you who are blind!"

Conclusion

Von Balthasar believes that Mechthild stands between
Hildegard and Eckhart, representing the best of mystical theology in the Middle Ages. He laments the fact that in the seven
hundred years that separate Mechthild from the twentieth
century there has been no serious theological study of her
work. We now have Frank Tobin's fine English translation of
The Flowing Light of the Godhead and a host of interpretative
studies such as those represented in the footnotes. There is no
excuse for our entering the next millennium of the Church
bereft of the light that comes to us from Mechthild's *Flowing
Light.*

1 *Mechthild of Magdeburg: The Flowing Light of the Godhead,* translated and introduced by
   Frank J. Tobin, preface by Margot Schmidt, New York-Mahwah: Paulist Press, 1998.
   (Henceforth, *Flowing*).
2 Bernard McGinn, *The Flowering of Mysticism: Men and Women in the New Mysticism,*
   1200–1350, New York: Crossroad, 1998, p. 223.

Mechthild of Magdeburg

3 *Flowing,* 2:26, p. 96.

4 Op. cit., p. 225.

5 Von Balthasar's celebrated essay, "The Ecclesial Mission of Mechthild," is not easily available, and I am reliant upon the substantial use made of it in Emilie Zum Brunn and Georgette Epiney-Burgard, *Women Mystics in Medieval Europe,* (tr. S. Hughes), New York: Paragon House, 1989, pp. 40–42, here p. 41. Frank Tobin considers this essay by von Balthasar "the most thoughtful and sensitive evaluation of Mechthild and her book in the postwar period. . . ." See his *Mechthild von Magdeburg: A Medieval Mystic in Modern Eyes,* Columbia SC: Camden House, Inc., 1995, p. 60.

6 *Flowing,* 7:3, p. 277.

7 Ibid., 7:46, p. 315.

8 Edith Scholl, "To Be a Full-Grown Bride: Mechthild of Magdeburg," in Lillian T. Shank and John A. Nichols, ed., *Peace Weavers,* Kalamazoo MI: Cistercian Publications, Inc., 1987, p. 225.

9 *Flowing,* 7:25, p. 295.

10 Ibid., 6:7, p. 234.

11 Ibid., 2:24, p. 90.

12 Ibid., 3:9, p. 114.

13 Scholl, op. cit., p. 225.

14 Op. cit., p. 239.

15 *Flowing,* 5:25, p. 207.

16 Tobin, op. cit., p. 62.

17 *Flowing,* 5:8, pp. 186–87.

18 Ibid., 2:4, p. 74. See also Ulrike Wiethaus, *Ecstatic Transformation: Transpersonal Psychology in the Work of Mechthild of Magdeburg,* Syracuse NY: Syracuse University Press, 1996, p. 136.

19 *Flowing,* 2:22, p. 87.

20 Ibid., 7:21, p. 293.

21 Ibid., 4:1, p. 141.

22 Ibid., 4:8, pp. 150–51.

23 Ibid., 2:7, p. 7.

24 Ibid., 6:36, pp. 261–62.

Chapter 5

Catherine of Siena

Francois Vandenbroucke, in his contribution "New Milieux, New Problems: From the Twelfth to the Sixteenth Century" in Louis Bouyer's magisterial *A History of Christian Spirituality,* opens his account of Saint Catherine of Siena with these words: "Catherine attracts us with a charm comparable with that of the Poor Man of Assisi, and this makes the historian's task more difficult."[1] To no small extent he is right. Our information about the life of Catherine of Siena is provided mainly by Blessed Raymond of Capua's biography of her, completed in 1395.[2] Although the biography is intended to be inspirational, and reflects the piety of the time with all its hagiographical and cultural assumptions, today the consensus of "Catherine scholars" is that it is largely accurate since Raymond was scholarly, having trained in theology at the University of Bologna. Much of our information will rely on Raymond's *Life of Catherine.*

Catherine was born in Siena in 1347, the twenty-third child of Jacopo Benincasa and his wife, Lapa Piagenti. Her father, a wool-dyer, was eventually supportive of her religious tendencies and vocation, but her mother has been described by Kenelm Foster, the English Dominican, as "spiritually rather obtuse."[3] Foster's description of Lapa seems somewhat harsh. Catherine was led to an intense religious and ascetic life, including a vow of virginity, as a result of a visionary experience of Christ when she was six. Undoubtedly, Lapa's negative reaction to her daughter's piety had to do more with a concern for her well-being than with an insensitivity to her spiritual progress.

Although able to read, it seems that Catherine had little in the way of formal education.[4] Three years of intense prayer and mystical experiences followed her becoming a Dominican tertiary, a member of the *Mantellate,* in 1364–65. The *Mantellate* were women associated with the Dominicans, wearing the Dominican habit but essentially living in their own homes. Her connection with the Dominicans was to be expected given that her family lived very near the church and cloister of San Domenico, the center in Siena of Dominican learning, preaching and spirituality. Her life then fell into three phases: from 1368 to the summer of 1374; from the summer of 1374 to November 1378; and the eighteen months until her death in 1380. During the first period, friends and disciples of both sexes, priests and laity, gathered around Catherine in Siena; this family of hers, the "Caterinati," even included an Augustinian friar from England, William Flete, who had a hermitage near Siena. During this time she dictated many letters dealing with spiritual matters, in which she was now an acknowledged leader, and also with public affairs. Almost 400 of her letters from this period have been collected and edited. Alice Curtayne, an author of an earlier generation and a biographer of Catherine, describes the shock of delight she received on first opening Catherine's letters:

> From that moment I was committed . . . the letters were fascinating: the forceful phrasing, the direct hitting, the genuineness of that devotion poured over and over again in a torrent. . . . I read through every page in the six volumes, copying into a notebook the passages that particularly appealed to me. For the first time in my life I was studying for the sheer love of it.[5]

While Curtayne's reaction is uniquely hers, it is not excessive. Kenelm Foster maintains that Catherine's letters bear comparison with the letters of Saint Paul.[6] Catherine was making a name for herself. However, her youth and the fact that she had no significant, official role in society attracted considerable negative attention. She made her first visit to Florence in 1374, in response to a summons to the general chapter of the

Dominican Order in that city.[7] Catherine gave a good account of herself and satisfied the Dominican authorities. Raymond of Capua, O.P., (1330–1399) was appointed director of both Catherine and her family of followers.

The second phase of Catherine's life, 1374–1378, witnessed her greatest influence on public affairs; it was also when she learned to write. Her impact and her public role are astonishing, given the social and cultural milieu in which she lived. It was very much a man's world and yet, as Jean Finley, O.P., points out, speaking of Catherine's entire life and not just this second phase, "Catherine was at ease in increasingly unfeminine roles, whether preaching to the Carthusian monks on the island of Gorgona or speaking words of comfort and hope to Pope Urban VI and his cardinals gathered in Rome to receive her in public audience."[8]

Two issues in particular engaged her attention: the crusade against the Turks and the war between Florence and her Italian allies against the papacy (1376–1378). Catherine advocated a crusade against the Turks because she believed such an enterprise would help unite a fragmenting Christendom, and also because if the Muslims were converted to Christ, "their new faith would be a leaven to reinvigorate a sick Church."[9] In June 1376, at the request of some Florentines, she went to Avignon, where the popes had been in residence since 1309, to meet Gregory XI, the last of the French popes, with the purpose of making peace between the pope and Florence. She failed, but she influenced Gregory to return with the Curia to Rome. In her correspondence with Gregory, Catherine calls him *dulcissimo babbo mio,* "my sweetest daddy," but in point of fact she could be quite exacting. For example, she writes to Gregory:

> Even if you have not been very faithful in the past, begin now to follow Christ, whose vicar you are, in real earnest. And do not be afraid. . . . Attend to things spiritual, appointing good shepherds and

rulers in the cities under your jurisdiction. . . .
Above all, delay no longer in returning to Rome
and proclaiming the Crusade.[10]

By January 1377 Catherine was back in Siena, and Gregory
was in Rome.

In March 1378 Gregory XI died and was succeeded that year by
Pope Urban VI). The late Anglican theologian and historian of
doctrine, Canon John N. D. Kelly, describes the uproar in
Rome prior to the election of Urban VI: "Dreading the election
of a Frenchman and the return of the papacy to Avignon,
excited crowds demonstrated in the streets and even invaded
the palace, clamouring for 'a Roman, at any rate an Italian,' as
pope."[11] In the fall of 1378, the Great Schism began. A number
of cardinals elected Clement VII as antipope, for all practical
purposes splitting the Church. Catholics looking back on this
difficult period of the Church's history accept that the "real"
popes were Urban VI and his successors, elected by his cardinals and their successors. In reality, however, it was far more
ambiguous. The Cambridge historian of the Church, Eamon
Duffy, describes the situation more accurately:

> At the time, however, and throughout the thirty-nine
> years during which the schism persisted, this sort of
> clarity was hard to come by. . . . Successive popes
> (five in all) and antipopes (four in all) expressed a
> wish to see the schism end, but in practice both sides
> put all their energies into consolidating their own
> support and undermining that of their rivals. For
> the Church at large it was a trauma.[12]

From November 1378 until her death in 1380 Catherine was in
Rome, summoned there by Urban VI. Her major public concern was pleading on behalf of Urban VI and the unity of the
Church. At the same time, her book, *The Dialogue,* was being
composed; it consisted of four treatises, "her spiritual testament to the world."[13] From the beginning of 1380, she was

unable to eat and her strength began quickly to fail. Until almost the end of February, she dragged herself the mile to St. Peter's each morning for Mass and remained in prayer in the basilica until vespers. She died in Rome on April 29, 1380, just thirty-three years old. In addition to her letters and *The Dialogue*, during the last three and a half years of her life, friends transcribed twenty-six of her prayers, spoken in ecstasy. She was canonized in 1461, and in 1970 Pope Paul VI named her Doctor of the Church.

Aspects of Her Teaching

Catherine was not a speculative or systematic theologian like the great medieval doctors. Her theology is best understood as an "intuitive grasp of what is essential in the Christian life, and flowing from that, her ability to offer new depths of insight into the central Christian mystery of God's love for humanity in Jesus Christ."[14] Although she certainly could read, she did not study theology from books and formal treatises but absorbed a rich knowledge of Scripture and a certain familiarity with patristic and medieval authors. Basic to her theology and spirituality is the Triune God. "The Trinity," writes Kenelm Foster, "underpins everything that St. Catherine says about the human soul and Christ."[15] Creation is the consequence of God's going out from himself in ecstatic love, sharing being with others. The human person, as the very climax of this creative, ecstatic love, is made in the image of the trinitarian God. When the soul becomes aware of God it simultaneously becomes aware of its own defects:

> As the soul comes to know herself she also knows God better, for she sees how good he has been to her. In the gentle mirror of God she sees her own dignity: that through no merit of hers but by his creation she is the image of God. And in the mirror of God's goodness she sees as well her own unworthiness, the work of her own sin. For just as you can better see the blemish on your face when you look at yourself in a mirror, so the soul who in true

> self-knowledge rises up with desire to look at her-
> self in the gentle mirror of God with the eyes of
> understanding sees all the more clearly her own
> defects because of the purity she sees in him.[16]

Not only, however, is the soul made by grace in the image of God, but God-in-Christ has become our image through the incarnation.

> O depth of love! What heart could keep from break-
> ing at the weight of your greatness descending to
> the lowliness of our humanity? We are your image,
> and now by making yourself one with us you have
> become our image, veiling your eternal divinity in
> the wretched cloud and dung heap of Adam. And
> why? For love! You, God, became human and we
> have been made divine![17]

The Eucharist

The Second Vatican Council said, "The Church has always venerated the divine Scriptures as she venerated the Body of the Lord, in so far as she never ceases, particularly in the sacred liturgy, to partake of the bread of life and to offer it to the faithful from the one table of the Word of God and the Body of Christ."[18] Taking this image of nourishment from the one table of the word of God and the body of Christ is a help-ful way in which to think about the meaning of the Eucharist for Catherine.

Catherine attended the Mass and the Divine Office daily for the most part. Throughout the course of the liturgical year, and many times over, she would have heard the psalms and the appointed readings from holy Scripture. Suzanne Noffke, O.P., the premier American expert on the work of Catherine, offers this observation: "It is my hunch . . . that Catherine's biblical allusions are drawn almost entirely from the selections to which she was regularly exposed in the liturgies of Mass and Office."[19] She would also have heard the scholarly preaching of the Dominicans of the Church of San Domenico, both at liturgy and in their various catechetical sessions as well as through instructions for the *Mantellate*. From all these forms of the "ministry of the Word" Catherine was nourished. In Catherine's day frequent communion was an exceptional favor, communion once a month being considered frequent enough.[20] Aware of the intensity of her eucharistic hunger, her director, Raymond of Capua, received permission from Pope Gregory XI for a priest to travel with Catherine to hear her confession and to give her communion daily.[21]

Catherine realized that no one is worthy to receive the Eucharist but this, in her judgment, should not bar people from receiving holy communion. She noted in a letter to her friend Ristoro Canigiani that even the greatest virtuous deeds in the world would still leave a person unworthy. "We are unworthy of God. But God is worthy of us and desires to give himself to us as food; with his own worth Jesus makes worthy those who desire him."[22] Her frequent spiritual advice to others who felt a sense of unworthiness before the Eucharist was this, Christ speaking to the soul: "But I am worthy that you should enter into me."[23] The advice is patterned after the prayer during the communion rite, "Lord, I am not worthy. . . . " Jesus "en-worths" us in himself, so to speak. For Catherine the Eucharist feeds us with the flame of divine love, so, "The one fire of love inflaming the blood of Christ becomes a fire burning in each of us individually and in all of us together, until the entire world grows to share in its light and warmth."[24]

Like Mechthild of Magdeburg in the previous century, Catherine realizes a deep association of the Trinity with the Eucharist. We receive "the whole of God" in communion. Thus, she hears God saying to her:

> When [the soul] receives this sacrament she lives
> in me and I in her. Just as the fish is in the sea and
> the sea in the fish, so am I in the soul and the soul

in me, the sea of peace. . . . When this appearance
of bread has been consumed, I leave behind the
imprint of my grace, just as a seal that is pressed
into warm wax leaves its imprint when it is lifted
off. Thus does the power of this sacrament remain
there in the soul; that is, the warmth of my divine
charity, the mercy of the Holy Spirit, remains
there. The light of my only-begotten Son's wisdom
remains there, enlightening the mind's eye.[25]

The whole of God, all the persons of the Trinity, are at work
through the Eucharist to bring the soul into union with the
whole of God, the mercy of the Holy Spirit and the wisdom of
the Son. The consequence of this graceful work of the Trinity
is like the existence of a fish in the sea. It is a daring metaphor.
Just as the fish requires the sea for existence, for life, so the
sea almost seems to require the fish. One has to say "almost"
because, strictly speaking, God needs no one and nothing. And
yet, the logic of ecstatic divine love leads to God's sharing
existence with creatures, and to intensifying that sharing
through the Eucharist, as his unique self-gift.

For Catherine this union with the Trinity is no private union,
cut off from the rest of the Church or the rest of humankind.
In Prayer 13 we read:

And just as you give me yourself by communicat-
ing to me the body and blood of your only begotten
Son, therein giving me all of God and all of
humanity, so boundless love, I ask you to communicate to me the mystic body of holy Church and
the universal body of Christianity.[26]

This is a plenary sense of communion of creation/
humankind with the Church, and of the Church with the
Eucharist, that is, the whole of God. It is so close in meaning
to that magnificent description of the Church in the Second
Vatican Council's *Constitution on the Church,* paragraph 1:

"The Church is, in Christ in the nature of sacrament — a sign and instrument, that is, of communion with God and of unity among all. . . ." For Catherine, although she does not put it like this in so many words, the Eucharist makes the Church, and the Church is *the* sign of communion with God and with all of God's creation. Love of the Church shines through much of her writings and her work.

Of course, the operative presupposition of this eucharistic vision is the sheer reality of Christ's eucharistic presence. Without this reality, the organic vision Catherine offers is a chimera, a wild or foolish idea. In Prayer 10, she waxes eloquently about the reality of the eucharistic presence:

> Just as you gave us yourself, wholly God and wholly human, so you left us all of yourself as food so that while we are pilgrims in this life we might not collapse in our weariness but be strengthened by you, heavenly food. O mercenary people! And what has God left you? He has left you himself, wholly God and wholly human, hidden under the whiteness of this bread.[27]

The repetition of "wholly God, wholly human" very clearly underscores the eucharistic presence. But it is as if she cannot leave this mystery alone. It is overwhelming, and so Catherine continues in the same prayer:

> O fire of love! Was it not enough to gift us with creation in your image and likeness, and to create us anew to grace in your Son's blood, without giving us yourself as food, the whole of divine being, the whole of God? What drove you? Nothing but your charity, mad with love as you are![28]

Gifted with existence in creation and with redemption in the sacrifice of the cross, "your Son's blood," we are finally gifted with "the whole of divine being" in the Eucharist. In this prayer Catherine emphasizes our human pilgrimage through life, sustained by "the heavenly food." One can almost imagine her priest-companion feeding her daily with the eucharistic food as she undergoes her ecclesial pilgrimages. There is an indissoluble bond between her passion for the Eucharist and for the unity of the Church.

Conclusion

Europe was blessed with mystics in the fourteenth century, including Henry Suso (c. 1295–1366), Johannes Tauler (c. 1300–1361), both Dominicans, and the anonymous author of *The Cloud of Unknowing*. However, the closest parallel to Catherine of Siena and her *Dialogue* was probably Julian of Norwich and her *Revelations*.[29] They make an interesting contrast. Catherine was not a nun, but as a Dominican tertiary lived an intensely religious life. In all likelihood, Julian was not a nun, but lived the life of an anchoress. Catherine was a very public person in fourteenth-century Italy, while Julian was a very private person in fourteenth-century England. Both share an intense love of the Eucharist. It is Julian who will be the subject of our next exploration.

[1] Jean Leclercq, Francois Vandenbroucke and Louis Bouyer, *The Spirituality of the Middle Ages*, (*A History of Christian Spirituality*, vol. 3), London: Burns and Oates, 1968, p. 409.

[2] Raymond, *The Life of Catherine of Siena*, tr. Conleth Kearns, O.P., Wilmington: Michael Glazier, 1980. Hereafter, *Life*.

[3] Kenelm Foster, "Catherine of Siena," *New Catholic Encyclopedia*, vol. 3, p. 258.

[4] C.H. Lawrence, "St. Catherine: Loving Critic," *The Tablet*, 234, 1980, p. 392.

[5] Walter Romig, ed., *The Book of Catholic Authors*, Detroit: W. Romig and Co., 1942, p. 128.

[6] "St. Catherine's Teaching on Christ," *Life of the Spirit*, 16, 1962, p. 311.

[7] See the discussion in *Catherine of Siena, The Dialogue*, Translation and introduction by Suzanne Noffke, O.P., Preface by Giuliana Cavallini, New York-Mahwah: Paulist Press, 1980, p. 5. Hereafter, *The Dialogue*.

[8] Jean Finley, O.P., *Catherine of Siena, Woman of Faith*, Sparkill NY: Convent of the Our Lady of the Rosary, 1980, p. 10.

[9] Suzanne Noffke, O.P., "Catherine of Siena," *The Encyclopedia of Religion*, vol. 3, p. 120.

[10] Kenelm Foster, O.P. and Mary J. Ronayne, ed., *I, Catherine: Selected Writings of Catherine of Siena*, London: Collins, 1980, p. 94.

[11] *The Oxford Dictionary of Popes*, Oxford and New York: Oxford University Press, 1986, p. 227.

[12] Eamon Duffy, *Saints and Sinners: A History of the Popes*, New Haven and London: Yale University Press, 1997, p. 127.

[13] Foster, "Catherine of Siena," p. 260.

[14] Mary O'Driscoll, O.P., "Catherine the Theologian," *Spirituality Today*, 40, 1988, p. 5; Suzanne Noffke, O.P., "Catherine of Siena: The Responsive Heart," in Annice Callahan, R.S.C.J., ed., *Spiritualities of the Heart*, New York-Mahwah: Paulist Press, 1990, p. 65; Vandenbroucke, op. cit., pp. 411–12.

[15] "St. Catherine's Teaching on Christ," p. 314.

[16] *The Dialogue*, 13, p. 48.

Catherine of Siena

[17] Ibid., p. 50.

[18] *Dei Verbum,* 21.

[19] Suzanne Noffke, O.P., *Catherine of Siena: Vision through a Distant Eye,* Collegeville MN: The Liturgical Press, 1996, p. 43.

[20] Mary J. Finnegan, "Catherine of Siena: The Two Hungers," *Mystics Quarterly,* 17, 1991, p. 176.

[21] Raymond, *Life,* 2.12.314, p. 291.

[22] Cited from Mary Ann Fatula, O.P., *Catherine of Siena's Way,* Wilmington DL: Michael Glazier, 1987, pp. 130–31.

[23] Ibid., p. 183.

[24] Ibid., p. 132.

[25] *The Dialogue,* 112, p. 211. See also Noffke, "Catherine of Siena: The Responsive Heart," p. 66.

[26] Suzanne Noffke, O.P., ed., *The Prayers of Catherine of Siena,* New York-Mahwah: Paulist Press, 1980, p. 108.

[27] Ibid., p. 78.

[28] Ibid., p. 79.

[29] Lawrence, op. cit., p. 392.

Chapter 6

Julian of Norwich

Julian was an anchoress attached to the Church of St. Julian in Norwich, in the southeast of England. An anchoress was one who retired from the world to live within the confines of her anchorhold, her church dwelling. An anchorhold was a fair-sized room or suite of rooms, often attached to the side of the church, as in Julian's circumstances. Usually there was a small window through the wall of the church so that the anchoress could follow the daily liturgy; there might also be a window to the world, so to speak, into a parlor for those who came for spiritual guidance.

Historically, the root of this impulse is in the tradition of the desert fathers and mothers, who went into the desert to be found by God, and so to find God and to be transformed by that finding. Theologically, then, the purpose was to set oneself apart for prayer and communion with God, to seek his presence and to develop holiness of life. An anchoress was expected to pray for the town in which she lived, a prime expression of her ecclesial unity with all the townsfolk and, ultimately, with all humankind. Here is no flight from the world in a negative sense of that word, but rather a being-for-the-world, a being in prayer before God for the world. Because of her vocation the anchoress was in an excellent position to offer spiritual counsel to those who sought it. We know that Julian offered such counsel and direction because she is mentioned in the *Book of Margery Kempe,* which narrates the mystical experiences of Margery Kempe (ca. 1373– after 1433) of King's Lynn, Norfolk — mystic, religious pilgrim to various shrines of Europe and mother of fourteen children. Kempe consulted Julian at her anchorhold ca. 1412 or 1413, demonstrating that Julian must have had a reputation for wise spiritual direction.

Our knowledge of Julian's life is scant. We do not even know her given name, Julian being the name of the church to which she was attached. She tells us in the Short Text of her *Revelations* that the "shewings" occurred to her on May 13, 1373, when she was thirty and a half years of age; this suggests that she was born in 1342. While the year of her death is unknown, it must have been after 1413, because in that year the author of the preface to the Short Text knows her to be still alive.[1] Some scholars, for example Joan Nuth, argue that Julian was a nun before becoming an anchoress, but I am convinced by the argument of the Anglican medieval historian Benedicta Ward, S.L.G., that this was not the case.[2] The church of St. Julian was under the patronage of Carrow Abbey, a Benedictine house just outside the city of Norwich. If Julian had been a nun of Carrow before becoming an anchoress at St. Julian's, one would expect to find some evidence of this in her writings; in point of fact, she never mentions nuns or monks, nor is she herself ever mentioned in any existing records of Carrow. Ward concludes that it is unlikely "that a nunnery with such a member, known in her own time as such an outstanding counselor and visionary, would not have done two things: made a fuss to ensure her burial in their grounds and boasted of it; and made sure of having copies made of her *Revelations* and both keeping them securely, and making them available."[3] In fact, Julian's work virtually disappeared because of the very few copies that appear to have been made.

Julian is mentioned in wills in Norwich, donors bequeathing to her various sums of money, again indicating something of the high esteem in which she was held. Although she probably lived into her seventies, the exact year of her death and the place of her burial are unknown. Grace Jantzen aptly comments, "No doubt she would have preferred it that way."[4]

Julian's Visions
When Julian was thirty and one-half years old, she became seriously ill. She received the last rites of the Church and grew increasingly weaker, but lingered for two more days and

nights. On the third night, it looked as though she was on the point of death, so that those who were with her, including her mother, sent for a priest so that he could be with her as she expired. The priest naturally brought with him a crucifix, which he placed before her eyes so that she might fix her gaze upon it to the end. This was the occasion of her *Revelations* on May 13, 1373, and she felt commanded to put them into writing. Her visions were, among other things, of Christ's loving suffering on the cross, and of creation as small as a hazelnut in one's hands yet utterly loved by God. She notes a certain parallel between herself and the Lord Jesus. Like Christ, she is 30 years old when she enters into her own particular passion and suffering. She suffers for three days and nights. Were her visions hallucinatory, perhaps brought on by her illness? This is the kind of question that a generation schooled in psychology might raise. Julian raised it herself:

> Then a man of religion came to me and asked me how I did, and I said that during the day I had been raving. And he laughed aloud and heartily. And I said: The cross that stood at the foot of my bed bled profusely; and when I said this, the religious I was speaking to became very serious and surprised. And at once I was very ashamed of my imprudence, and I thought: This man takes serious every word I could say, and he says nothing in reply. And when I saw that he treated it so seriously and so respectfully, I was greatly ashamed, and wanted to make my confession. . . .[5]

She felt herself to be somewhat ungrateful for trivializing in this way the experiences she had received, and so felt the need to confess her sin. Between the Short Text of the *Revelations* and the Long Text there are some twenty years, in which time Julian had an opportunity to probe their meaning and communicate it to others.

Julian's Theology

"Julian insists that all we can know about God is revealed to us in the person of Jesus. This means that the mystical life here on earth can never depart from the image of the crucified Jesus."[6] Her reflections on the Trinity are focused on the cross of Christ as the very expression of God's love for humankind. Her revelations vibrate from beginning to end with the theme, "Love was his meaning."

> And from the time it was revealed, I desired many times to know in what was our Lord's meaning. And fifteen years after and more, I was answered in spiritual understanding, and it was said: What, do you wish to know your Lord's meaning in this thing? Know it well, love was his meaning. Who reveals it to you? Love. What did he reveal to you? Love. Why does he reveal it to you? For love. Remain in this, and you will know more of the same. But you will never know different without end.[7]

The passion of Christ is itself understood as love, as the supreme manifestation of the love of God. For Julian, in a sense, love is a way of describing every attribute of God. Love is not something that God does, or expresses alongside other manifestations of his being. All God's actions and all God's being are integrated in love:

> Truth sees God, and wisdom contemplates God, and of these two comes the third, and that is a marvelous delight in God, which is love. Where truth and wisdom are, truly there is love, truly coming from them both, and all are of supreme wisdom, endless supreme wisdom uncreated; and a man's soul is a creature in God which has the same properties created. And always it does what it was created for; it sees God and it contemplates God and it loves God. Therefore, God rejoices in the creature

and the creature in God, endlessly marveling, in which marveling he sees his God, his Lord, his maker, so exalted, so great and so good in comparison with him who is made that the creature scarcely seems anything to itself. But the brightness and clearness of truth and wisdom make him see and know that he is made for love, in which God endlessly protects him.[8]

It is a splendid reflection on the insight of St. John, "God is love and those who abide in love abide in God, and God in them" (1 John 4:16).

Julian associates power with the Father, wisdom with the Son, and goodness with the Holy Spirit; yet she recognizes that each of their attributes belongs to each of the persons of the undivided Trinity. It is helpful for us to think of the divine attributes separately, but Julian realizes full well that the mystery of the Trinity cannot be separated:

And our substance is in our Father, God almighty, and our substance is in our Mother, God all Wisdom, and our substance is in our Lord God, the Holy Spirit, all goodness, for our substance is whole in each person of the Trinity, who is one God.[9]

In this lovely passage, Julian speaks of Christ as our Mother, and to this profound theme we must now turn our attention.

Christ Our Mother

In Julian's conception of the motherhood of God we find some of her most original and profound teaching, yet her attribution of maternal qualities to God as such or to the person of Christ is not especially novel.[10] Suggestions of divine motherhood can be found in Holy Scripture. Think of the image of the Spirit of God hovering over the face of the deep in Genesis as a maternal image, as of a hen hovering and brooding over her chicks (Genesis 1:2). (Admittedly, newer translations of the Bible often have other forms of expression here such as "a mighty wind swept over the waters" *[New American Bible]*. Such translations are unfortunate, and I find myself entirely in agreement with Geoffrey Wainwright when he says of them, "To stay at that level would be a reductive translation, disallowing the divine reference of the analogy and running counter to the point of the story of creation as God's work."[11]) Consider also the magnificent passage in Isaiah 49:15, "Can a woman forget her sucking child, that she would have no compassion on the son of her womb? Even these may forget, yet I will not forget you."

Closer to Julian's own time, similar maternal imagery is found the writings of Anselm of Canterbury, who saw the passion of Christ in terms of motherhood: "As a mother is in labor to bring forth her children, so Christ is in labor on the cross to give spiritual birth to those who would be called by his name."[12] Because of the considerable influence Anselm had in England, it is just possible that Julian had come across in him this maternal image of Jesus. It is perhaps noteworthy that the idea of divine motherhood does not occur in the Short Text; only after long meditation does it emerge.

In Julian motherhood is attributed not only to Christ but also to the Church:

> With this I am well satisfied, waiting upon our Lord's will in this great marvel. And now I submit myself to my mother, Holy Church, as a simple child should.[13]

The Church as mother is, of course, commonplace in the Christian tradition since at least the time of Saint Cyprian of Carthage, who held that one "cannot have God for his Father who does not have the Church for his Mother."[14] For Julian, the Church is not something other than or independent of Christ. The Church is Christ's Body. "It is, therefore," as Grace

Jantzen has it, "a very short step from thinking of the Church as our Mother to thinking of Christ as our Mother."[15] Julian continues in this vein at some length with much spiritual insight.

> The mother may sometimes suffer the child to fall and be distressed in various ways for its own benefit, but she can never suffer any kind of peril to come to her child, because of her love. And though our earthly mother may suffer her child to perish, our Heavenly Mother Jesus may never suffer us who are his children to perish, for he is almighty, all wisdom and all love, and so is none but he, blessed may he be. But often when our falling and wretchedness are shown to us, we are so much afraid and so greatly ashamed of ourselves that we scarcely know where we can put ourselves. But then our courteous Mother does not wish us to flee away, for nothing would be less pleasing to him; but he then wants us to behave like a child. For when it is distressed and frightened, it runs quickly to its mother; and, if it can do no more, it calls to the mother for help with all its might. So, he wants us to act like a meek child and say: My kind Mother, my gracious Mother, my Beloved Mother, have mercy on me.[16]

Jesus is our Mother. The Church is our Mother, too. Here is a fine example of a Pauline insight coming to fruition in Julian, that is to say, "No Christ without the Church; no Church without Christ." This image is explored more profoundly when she speaks of the Eucharist.

The Eucharist

Throughout her *Revelations* Julian constantly alludes to the rites of the Church. Belief in the seven sacraments is part of her Christian faith, as she tells us in the Long Text: "In our faith come the seven sacraments, one following another in the order God has ordained them in for us, and every kind of virtue."[17] This is what one would expect of an orthodox Christian of the time.

In contrast to some of the other women mystics and visionaries considered in our series, Julian writes very little about the Eucharist, but what she has to say is particularly beautiful. In the sixtieth chapter of the Long Text occurs the only passage where Julian speaks of the Eucharist. To open up her understanding it is necessary to turn first to the entire chapter, in which she is contemplating the motherhood of God at work. We have seen something of the power and beauty of this image for Julian. For her there simply is no other human relationship that comes closer to expressing God's love for us than motherhood. The image is so organic and all-encompassing for her that she can apply it to Mary, the Church and our natural mothers, as well as to Jesus. This complex referral of the mother image can be frustrating to systematic theologians, heaven bent on analysis. A consistently linear referral would be so much clearer. The very value of imaging God as Mother for Julian becomes its sheer polyvalence, its ability to encapsulate a range of meanings, deeply focused on God's own self.

> How we are brought back by the motherhood of
> mercy and grace into our natural place, in which
> we were created by the motherhood of love, a moth-
> er's love that never leaves us.[18]

Unlike our earthly mothers who "bear us for pain and death," our true Mother Jesus "bears us for joy and for endless life."[19] We share that joy and endless life when we are brought to birth by Mother Jesus, and the labor pains of Mother Jesus are the pain and suffering of the cross. From Jesus' writhing in travail upon the cross the Church is born.

A child once born needs to be fed and nourished, and Julian tells us that Mother Jesus feeds us with his own self. The passage is very lovely and needs to be quoted at some length:

Julian of Norwich

The mother can give her child to suck of her milk, but our precious Mother Jesus can feed us with himself, and does, most courteously and most tenderly, with the blessed sacrament, which is the precious food of true life; and with all the sweet sacraments he sustains us most mercifully and graciously, and so he meant in these blessed words, where he said: I am he whom Holy Church preaches and teaches to you. That is to say: All the health and life of the sacraments, all the power and grace of my word, all the goodness which is ordained in Holy Church for you, I am he.[20]

Here is a most powerful image of eucharistic ecclesiology. The Eucharist makes the Church, the Church is Christ, fed by Christ. Julian takes the image even further:

The mother can lay her child tenderly to her breast, but our tender Mother Jesus can lead us easily into his blessed breast through his sweet open side, and show us there a part of the godhead and of the joys of heaven, with inner certainty of endless bliss.[21]

She is thinking here of Christ's side opened by the lance on Calvary. The sacred wound becomes the maternal entry point to the within of his breast in which we behold his divine glory. This divine glory is also the Church's. We are called and invited to participate in it. While this is a very lofty view of the Church, Julian realizes that the Church on earth, despite these wondrous sacramental means, is imperfect. Our human performance, under grace, remains always flawed until the end.[22] The process of divinization, essential to which is also the sacrament of penance, continues until the final in-gathering at the end-time.

Conclusion

Julian of Norwich was a mystic. There is an approach to mysticism today which sees the doctrines of the Church, the tradition of the Church and the language of Christian theology as so many "wrappings" for mystical experience. The wrappings are not central or essential. For example, Karen Armstrong writes: "In recent years people have found the doctrines of Christianity increasingly difficult, but a visionary like Julian penetrates the cerebral crust of the religious experience which has little to do with logic and reason, to its core."[23] The approach to Julian here is the opposite of Armstrong's. It is precisely through her profound appreciation of the doctrines of her faith that Julian's mystical theology finds expression: through Christ and the Trinity, through the Church and the Eucharist, through a life of prayer shaped by the doctrinal tradition of the Church. Julian is a mystic, not in spite of doctrinal traditions, but through them. One author puts it astutely like this: "The intellectual apprehension of doctrine is not, for Julian, a 'crust' over religious experience; rather, it is like a knife she wields to prune and probe her revelation."[24] We find in Julian no encouragement for an amorphous Christianity that sits ill at ease with its tradition and the institutional dimension of Catholicism. It is because she knows and loves the tradition of Eucharist that she has received that she is able to soar in her eucharistic images. That is part of her special gift to the Church of today: Know the tradition, live that tradition, explore the tradition imaginatively, and through that knowing and imaginative exploring, "tradition" it to others.

1 Edmund Colledge, O.S.A., and James Walsh, S.J., ed., *Julian of Norwich, Showings,* New York-Ramsey-Toronto: Paulist Press, 1978, p. 125. The Short Text will be referred to as ST and the Long Text as LT, followed by the chapter and page number in the Colledge-Walsh edition.

2 Joan M. Nuth, *Wisdom's Daughter: The Theology of Julian of Norwich,* New York: Crossroad, 1991, pp. 9–10; Kenneth Leech and Benedicta Ward, S.L.G., *Julian Reconsidered,* Fairacres, Oxford: S.L.G. Press, 1988, p. 21.

3 Ibid., p. 21.

4 Grace M. Jantzen, *Julian of Norwich, Mystic and Theologian,* London: S.P.C.K., 1987, 59.

5 ST 21, p. 162.

6 Bernard McGinn, "Medieval English Mystics," in Jill Raitt, ed., *Christian Spirituality: High Middle Ages and Reformation,* New York: Crossroad, 1988, p. 204.

Julian of Norwich

[7] LT 86, p. 342.

[8] LT 45, p. 256.

[9] LT 58, p. 295.

[10] A fine treatment of this theme may be found in Caroline Walker Bynum, *Jesus as Mother: Studies in the Spirituality of the High Middle Ages,* Berkeley, Los Angeles, London: University of California Press, 1982, pp. 110–69.

[11] In his essay, "The Holy Spirit," in Colin E. Gunton, ed., *The Cambridge Companion to Christian Doctrine,* Cambridge: Cambridge University Press, 1997, p. 274.

[12] From Saint Anselm's "Prayer to St. Paul," cited in Jantzen, op. cit., pp. 117–18.

[13] LT 46, p. 259.

[14] Saint Cyprian, "On the Unity of the Church," cited in John N. D. Kelly, *Early Christian Doctrines,* rev. ed., San Francisco: HarperCollins, 1978, p. 206.

[15] Op. cit., p. 119.

[16] LT 61, p. 301.

[17] LT 57, p. 292.

[18] LT 60, p. 297.

[19] LT 60, p. 298.

[20] Ibid.

[21] Ibid.

[22] See LT, 61–63, pp. 299–305.

[23] Karen Armstrong, *Visions of God: Four Medieval Mystics and Their Writings,* New York: Bantam Books, 1994, p. 177. I owe this reference and this point to the work of Frederick Bauerschmidt.

[24] Frederick C. Bauerschmidt, "Julian of Norwich — Incorporated," *Modern Theology,* 13, 1997, p. 81. See also Nuth, op. cit., pp. 23–24.

Chapter 7

Catherine of Genoa

Blessed Julian of Norwich makes a sharp contrast with Catherine of Genoa. Julian was an anchoress, living in the city of Norwich, praying on behalf of that city but far from the madding crowd. Catherine was a married woman, living in the city of Genoa, working on behalf of that city's sick and poor in the very midst of the madding crowd. Both were laywomen, mystics, who were marked by a profound sense of union with Christ and who placed the Eucharist central in their spirituality.

Saint Catherine of Genoa was born Caterinetta Fieschi, of a noble Genovese family in the fall of 1447. Her father, Giacomo Fieschi, who died in 1461, had been viceroy of Naples. At the age of sixteen she married Giuliano Adorno, a marriage apparently arranged by her oldest brother, Giacomo. The Adorno and Fieschi families had been enemies, and the marriage was arranged for financial and political motives.[1] Giuliano was unfaithful to her, had a mistress and child, and neglected her. After ten years in an unhappy marriage, and suffering from acute depression, Catherine experienced a conversion at age 26 on the occasion of her Lenten confession March 22, 1473. As a result of this conversion experience, Catherine undertook personal penance, spent extended time in prayer and meditation, and began to devote her life to the poor and marginal of the city of Genoa. Friedrich Von Hugel, who wrote the classic study of Catherine in the twentieth century, says of this experience: "If the tests of reality in such things are their persistence and large and rich spiritual applicability and fruitfulness, then something profoundly real and important took place in the soul of that sad and weary woman."[2] She became a daily communicant, something very

Catherine of Genoa

rare for a laywoman in those days, and began to nurse the sick in the Pammatone, Genoa's largest hospital, which survived until the 1944 bombing of the Second World War.[3]

Giuliano's lifestyle reduced him to bankruptcy and poverty; unexpectedly, he had a similar conversion experience and with Catherine served the sick in the Pammatone hospital. They lived in continence first in a house near the hospital and later, in 1479, in two rooms within the hospital itself. According to Von Hugel, about this time Catherine became aware of her husband's mistress and of their child, Thobia.[4] She was concerned in a practical way for the welfare of this child. Benedict Groeschel comments on Catherine's reaction to Giuliano's bankruptcy and Thobia: "Catherine's accept-ance of this child and her forgiveness of her husband goes as much against the attitudes of her culture as does her response to Giuliano's bankruptcy."[5] In Genoa at this time bankruptcy was, seemingly, "the ultimate disgrace." Not only did Catherine stand alongside Giuliano in coping with this social and public humiliation, but she also provided financially for his child. Such commitment is as hard to find now as then. Their living in a continent marriage probably reflects their joint desire to live for God alone, as it were. At the same time, I cannot help but think that, while Catherine remained com-mitted to Giuliano, he was not her life-companion chosen out of a deep, personal and mutual love. Eventually he was to become a Franciscan tertiary, though Catherine did not follow in his footsteps.

The year 1493 was of particular significance for Catherine. From 1493 she developed a close friendship with a Genovese lawyer, Ettore Vernazza; it is from him that we obtain much of our information about Catherine's life. This young man, wealthy in his own right, was to spend himself in the service of the poor; he was the founder of the Oratory of Divine Love.

Catherine and Vernazza became associated during the plague that struck Genoa in 1493, when it is estimated that four-fifths of the people who remained in the city died. In the open area behind the hospital, Catherine set up a sort of field hospital to attend to the needs of the sick and the dying.

Strangely, until 1499 Catherine had no formal spiritual direction and seldom went to confession. In that year she found a priest, Cataneo Marabotto, who became her director and confessor. Beginning on March 25, 1476, and going on through the next 23 years, Catherine fasted during Advent and Lent; the fasts were not penitential in character, nor does she appear to have suffered excessive discomfort from them. The first account of her ecstasies occurred during this period of the fasting. In 1509 she began to experience the "flashes or fires of Divine Love."[6] Next to the experience of her conversion, these particularly intense mystical experiences of union with God are the most important of Catherine's life. After much suffering, as a result perhaps of a gastric cancer, Catherine died on Sunday, September 15, 1510.

Her Teaching

Everything we know of Catherine's life and teaching comes from three sources: the *Vita (Life)*, or biography, of Catherine; the *Trattato*, referred to here as *Purgation and Purgatory;* and the *Dialogo (Spiritual Dialogue)*. Catherine wrote none of these sources as such; they are interpretations of her teachings. All subsequent biographies and editions of her work are based ultimately on the *Life and Teachings* approved for publication by the Dominican, Geronimo of Genoa, in 1551. The *Life*, or biography, of Catherine, was probably compiled by her spiritual director, Marabotto, and her close friend, Vernazza. *Purgation and Purgatory* is an anthology of sayings and teachings on spiritual purgation, both in this life and in the next. Undoubtedly, some of this work contained interpretive glosses inserted before it was presented to the Dominican inquisitor prior to the official publication in 1551. *The Spiritual Dialogue* represents Catherine's own spiritual history in a more readable and accessible form.

Catherine of Genoa

Catherine was never a student of theology in any ordinary sense of the term. Her teaching is an expression of her own mystical experiences, perceptions and meditations. Donald Nugent puts it nicely: "The thing to bear in mind is that what we have with Catherine is not a theological system, but a theological life."[7] The magisterial study of Catherine undertaken by Von Hugel early in the twentieth century, however, points to three specific sources for her teaching.[8] The first source is the Bible, especially the prophet Isaiah, Psalms, and the Pauline and Johannine literature. The second source is the famous praise-poems of the Franciscan Jacopone da Todi (1228–1306). The third source appears to be the Christian-Neoplatonic works of Pseudo-Denis, a constant source of an influence upon Christian mystical writing. A contemporary of Catherine's, Marsilio Ficino, published a Latin translation of and commentary upon Pseudo-Denis's two books, *The Mystical Theology* and *The Divine Names,* in 1492.[9] In short, Catherine's spirituality and theological reflection were nourished by Scripture and the popular devotional literature of her time.

What are the principal themes of her teaching? Groeschel helpfully summarizes them as follows: God, the creator of all life, as pure Love and the total fulfillment of the rational soul; the soul, and the lifelong conflict between self love and pure love; the spiritual combat, in which the soul is only victorious through the grace of pure love; the outcome of the conflict, the last things.[10]

God reaches out to the soul as pure Love: "As for paradise, God has placed no doors there. Whoever wishes to enter, does so. All-merciful God stands there with his arms open, waiting to receive us into his glory."[11] Here is a mighty expression of God as Love, welcoming and wanting all of his human creatures. It is an expression of the great Platonic-Christian understanding that all reality proceeds from God in creation, and returns to God in redemption-consummation. "The soul which came out from God pure and full has a natural instinct to return to

God as full and pure [as it came]."[12] Catherine does not here believe in the pre-existence of souls when she says, "The soul which came out from God. . . ." Rather, this is her way of emphasizing that the soul has an innate sense of and desire for God as its fulfillment. She puts it like this in her *Purgation and Purgatory:*

> Joy in God, oneness with Him, is the end of these
> souls, an instinct implanted in them at their cre-
> ation. No image or metaphor can adequately con-
> vey this truth.[13]

I think Catherine shows herself aware of her daring language, but requires this daring language to be adequate to her mystical insights. Through God's graceful initiative, the soul is enabled to seek union with him. This seeking is a way or a process by which the soul is constantly striving for perfection, but the striving itself is understood as God's work in the soul. In a word, God is the true and authentic center of every person:

> My Me is God, nor do I recognize any other Me,
> except my God Himself. My Being is God, not by
> some simple participation but by a true transfor-
> mation of my Being.[14]

This is strong language indeed. Stronger still are these expressions:

> I will have nothing to do with a love that would be
> for God or in God; this is a love which pure love
> cannot bear: since pure love is [simply] God him-
> self; I cannot abide to see that word for, and that
> word in, since they denote to my mind a something
> that can stand between God and myself.[15]

That long-term student of Christian mysticism, Louis K. Dupre, has wisely written of mystical language like this: "To interpret [these] utterances as straightforward ontological propositions is to run into insurmountable difficulties. Most of those difficulties vanish if the emotive import of statements that may at first appear to have only cognitive purport be taken into consideration."[16] Dupre is suggesting that a literal reading of Catherine's language, for example, simply gets us into difficulties regarding God's existence and ours, and that a more adequate reading will take into account the emotive or intentional context of the language. That gloss of Dupre helps, but I would not wish to evacuate Catherine's language, nor the language of mystics in general, of ontological value. While the language is very strong, almost at times pantheistic, it seems to me that Catherine's meaning is little more than an articulation of what is implied in the first Letter of St. John, that "God is love, and those who abide in love abide in God and God in them" (1 John 4:16).

To achieve this unity with the Divine Love, the soul has to struggle to overcome the false love or the false self. Catherine is no spiritual romantic who thinks this unification just "happens." The struggle is constant; this constancy is understood by her to be a habit of purgation (the action of the soul), which is at the same time the act of being purged (the action of the God who is Love). If the purgation remains incomplete in this life, then it must continue after death, in the state of purgatory. Clearly there is no extrinsicism in Catherine's understanding of purgation/purgatory; it is the ineluctable movement of the soul intent on union with the Love/God. We could say that purgatory is a christological moment, the penultimate moment of our human participation in the Paschal Mystery of Christ, our final dying to self (that is, to what is not of Love/God), to be raised to our real self in Love/God. This is actually the fourth main element of Catherine's teaching: the outcome of the conflict, the last things and, especially, purgatory. Purgatory is not a *postmortem* punishment for sin external to the subject visited upon him/her by a God intent on justice; it is the working out of love (the subject) with Love (God).

[God] tugs at the soul with a glance, draws it and binds it to Himself with a fiery love that by itself could annihilate the immortal soul. In so acting, God so transforms the soul in Him that it knows nothing other than God; and He continues to draw it up into His fiery love until He restores it to that pure state from which it first issued. . . . The overwhelming love of God gives [the soul] a joy beyond words.[17]

The Scottish theologian D.W.D. Shaw, Professor of Divinity at the University of St. Andrews, had a saying, "Love is the logic of the universe."[18] Catherine understood this — in point of fact, this is *precisely* her understanding of purgatory — though she would probably not have expressed herself in this fashion. As Groeschel puts it, "The teaching on purgatory is . . . Catherine's great contribution to our understanding of eschatology."[19] Her doctrine on purgatory was to inspire John Henry Newman's great epic poem, *The Dream of Gerontius.*

Discussing Catherine's psychological state, Groeschel, a trained psychologist as well as theologian, points out that Catherine's outgoing personality, her ability to relate to an antagonistic husband, even her skepticism about the value of her fasts, do not paint a psychotic picture. At the same time, he notes: "Her depression and the voluntary attempts to overcome this state caused by her loneliness and solitude in the first years of her unhappy marriage suggest a more normal neurotic response to this genuinely miserable situation."[20]

Eucharist

Catherine has been described as a woman "in whose piety fasting, eucharist, and suffering were the central foci,"[21] and her spirituality as "eucharistic, ascetic, apophatic and mystical."[22] We have seen something of these various aspects of her life and spirituality; now it remains to probe her eucharistic spirituality.

Catherine of Genoa

From March 25, 1474, Catherine received the Eucharist almost daily — as already noted, a rare practice for a laywoman in the later Middle Ages. On that day "her Lord gave her the desire of holy communion, a desire which never again failed her throughout the whole course of her remaining life."[23] In the *Spiritual Dialogue* we get a clear sense of its importance for Catherine:

> To the last she always received the Eucharist. If she could not, that gave her more suffering than the illness. The day she did not receive communion she was hungry all day long. It seemed that she could not live without the sacrament.[24]

The last four months of her life were filled with suffering, so that she was unable to eat, but we are told: "She never had trouble, however, in receiving communion. . . . Completely in charge of her person, the Spirit left her only the instinct for the sacrament, which was never taken away from her."[25] Almost one month to the day before she died, on August 14, 1510, we are told the following:

> When she was about to receive communion at the usual time, she spoke such loving words to the sacrament that many present wept. In the presence of the Blessed Sacrament she was often passionately inspired, for her great and unutterable love for it penetrated to the deepest part of herself.[26]

On the very day she died, September 14, 1510, her companions asked her if she wished to receive holy communion.

> She answered by asking whether it was the usual time, and then pointed her finger toward heaven. The gesture implied that she was to receive communion in heaven, where she would be perpetually united to that sweet sacrament and her loving God.[27]

One author, noting that Catherine of Genoa is not as well known as her earlier namesake, Catherine of Siena, suggests two reasons. The first has to do with the many sainted Catherines of the sixteenth century, and the second has to do with the fact that "no astonishing miracles are attributed to her."[28] Perhaps this is too weak a definition of miracle. Perhaps the truly wonderful — "miracle" means literally a "wonderful action" — is the centrality of the Eucharist in her life, bringing her to a sense of union with God.

Conclusion

The Oratory of Divine Love was a sixteenth century reform movement in the Church in Italy, inspired by Catherine and founded by her close friend, Ettore Vernazza. Out of it came a number of significant Church reformers such as Pope Paul IV. Catherine's inspirational role in the origins of the Oratory of Divine Love has been described as the beginning of "the effective reform of the Catholic Church."[29] This is a remarkable statement with which to end our account of Catherine of Genoa. At the very moment when the Church, the Body of Christ, was being rent asunder in the direction of a particular kind of reform, the Eucharist being often the center of dispute, Catherine was giving rise to another kind of reform. This reform was not only from within the Church but also from within the spiritual life rooted in and founded on the Eucharist.

1 Benedict J. Groeschel, O.F.M.Cap., in *Catherine of Genoa: Purgation and Purgatory, The Spiritual Dialogue,* Translation and notes by Serge Hughes, Introduction by Benedict J. Groeschel, O.F.M.Cap., Preface by Catherine De Hueck Doherty, New York-Ramsey-Toronto: Paulist Press, 1979, p. 3. This is the text of Catherine used throughout, hereafter referred to as *Catherine.*

2 Friedrich Von Hugel, *The Mystical Element of Religion as Studied in Saint Catherine of Genoa and Her Friends,* 2 vols., London: E. J. Dent, 1908. Here, vol. 2, p. 29.

3 Kenelm Foster, O.P., "Catherine of Genoa," in Gordon S. Wakefield, ed., *A Dictionary of Christian Spirituality,* London: SCM Press, 1983, p. 80.

4 Von Hugel, op. cit., vol. 1, p. 129.

5 Groeschel, *Catherine,* p. 4.

6 The words are Groeschel's, *Catherine,* p. 18.

7 Donald C. Nugent, "The Annihilation of St. Catherine of Genoa," *Mystics Quarterly,* 10, 1984, p.170.

8 Von Hugel's work on Catherine has been described by Evelyn Underhill and Morton Kelsey as the greatest work on mysticism in English in the twentieth century. See Donald C. Nugent, op. cit., p. 182

9 Following Groeschel, *Catherine,* p. 24.

Catherine of Genoa

[10] Ibid., p. 27.

[11] Ibid., p. 78.

[12] *Life,* as cited in Friedrich Von Hugel, op. cit. vol. 1, p. 265.

[13] Groeschel, *Catherine,* p. 76.

[14] *Life,* as cited in Friedrich Von Hugel, op. cit., vol. 1, p. 265.

[15] Ibid., p. 266.

[16] Louis K. Dupre, *The Other Dimension: A Search for the Meaning of Religious Attitudes,* New York: Seabury Press, 1979, p. 357.

[17] Groeschel, *Catherine,* pp. 79–81.

[18] I owe this reference to Seymour House, who had been a student of Shaw's at the University of St. Andrews.

[19] Groeschel, *Catherine,* p. 34.

[20] Ibid., p. 9. Groeschel continues to provide helpful psychological commentary on Catherine, pp. 9–14.

[21] Caroline Walker Bynum, *Holy Feast and Holy Fast,* Berkeley-Los Angeles-London: University of California Press, 1987, p. 181.

[22] Nugent, op. cit., p. 183.

[23] *Life,* as cited in Friedrich Von Hugel, op. cit., vol. 1, p. 113.

[24] Groeschel, *Catherine,* p. 133.

[25] Ibid., p. 135.

[26] Ibid., p. 141.

[27] Ibid., p. 149.

[28] Donald C. Nugent, "Saint Catherine of Genoa," in Katharina M. Wilson, ed., *Women Writers of the Renaissance and Reformation,* Athens and London: University of Georgia Press, 1987, p. 68.

[29] John C. Olin, *The Catholic Reformation: Savonarola to Ignatius Loyola,* New York: Harper and Row, 1969, pp. 16–17. See also H. Outram Evenett, *The Spirit of the Counter Reformation,* Notre Dame and London: University of Notre Dame Press, 1968, p. 26.

Chapter 8

Teresa of Avila

If Saint Catherine of Genoa as a laywoman was to contribute to the reform of the Church through her influence on the Oratory of Divine Love, Saint Teresa of Avila as a religious was to do so through her religious foundations. Born in Avila in 1515, the year in which Martin Luther had the famous Tower experience that set him off in a reforming direction, Teresa de Ahumada lived her entire life in Castile, Spain.[1] During the sixteenth century, Spain experienced a spiritual revival not unlike that of the Flemish and German regions in the thirteenth and fourteenth centuries, some of which has been discussed in earlier essays. Louis Bouyer compares Teresa with Hadewijch of Antwerp, noting that yet again the spiritual initiative comes from a woman.[2]

Teresa's life has been thoroughly documented, and so only the bare outline will be presented here. In sixteenth-century Spain, "purity of blood" was an obsession.[3] Recent research has established that Teresa had Jewish blood. Her father and her grandfather, silk merchants in Toledo, were *Judeoconversos,* converts from Judaism; having done public penance in 1485, they moved to Avila after purchasing false certificates that acknowledged them as "Old Christians," men of honor and pure blood. It remains unclear whether Teresa knew about this or not. Most religious orders of the time did not permit anyone with mixed blood, either Jewish or Moorish, to enter.

The family was wealthy and Teresa enjoyed the benefits, living a fairly carefree life. Eventually, her father boarded her with the Augustinian nuns in Avila for a period of about 18 months. This proved a turning point for her. After a period of illness ending with convalescence in the home of an uncle who had a good library, Teresa decided to enter religious life. She entered the Carmelite Convent of the Incarnation in Avila in 1536, a time when the rule was not especially demanding. Her stay in the convent was interrupted by periods of illness, depression and frustration, which lasted until about 1554, when she experienced a conversion. This occurred while she was reading the *Confessions* of St. Augustine. Discipline and prayer, culminating in mystical experiences, shaped the rest of her life.

For the next seven years Teresa continued to live at the Convent of the Incarnation, but in 1562 she established the new, reformed Convent of St. Joseph in Avila, the first convent of Discalced, that is, unshod, Carmelites under a strictly reformed rule. The way of life was much more rigorous than it had been at the Convent of the Incarnation. The following five years were probably the most peaceful of her life. The Carmelite leaders approved the extension of her work in 1567, and by the time of her death she had founded twenty more convents. Her major writings include *The Way of Perfection,*[4] which is an explanation of prayer; *The Interior Castle,*[5] describing the dimensions of spiritual and mystical growth, and her *Life.*[6] She died in 1582 on her way home to Avila from making her last foundation in Burgos. She was made Doctor of the Church in 1970 by Pope Paul VI.

Mysticism and Spirituality

There is a well-known definition of mental prayer in Teresa's *Life:*

> Mental prayer in my opinion is nothing but an intimate sharing between friends; it means taking time frequently to be alone with him who we know loves us.[7]

According to Teresa more women than men receive mystical gifts:

There are many more women than men to whom
the Lord grants these favors. This I heard from the
saintly Friar Peter of Alcantara — and I too have
observed it — who said that women make much
more progress along this path than men do. He
gave excellent reasons for this, all in favor of
women; but there's no need to mention them here.[8]

The Interior Castle expresses for Teresa how God is calling and
working in the life of the soul. The journey into the interior of
the castle may be imaged as the movement from the circumference of a circle to its center. This particular geometric
image is more helpful than others because "the movement is
within, to a God who is always present."[9] At the same time,
this movement from the circumference to the center, to union
with the God who is always present, involves a correlative
growth in self-knowledge. The journey occurs through seven
stages or seven mansions.

The first dwelling place or mansion sets out the requirements
for the life of sanctity: purification from sin, worldly affairs
and pleasures; and prayer, which is the door of the castle (1, 1,
7; 2, 1, 11). The key at this stage of the spiritual life is intro-
spection and self-knowledge, but with the vision centered on
"Christ our good, from whom we shall learn true humility, and
also upon his saints" (1, 2, 11). The second mansion involves an
intensification of this pattern, as the soul receives the favor of
the Lord inviting it into relationship with him. The invitation
may come through conversations with others, sermons, spiritual reading, sickness, difficulties or prayer (2, 1, 2–3).
Struggle with the devil is part and parcel of this second mansion, testing the soul's resolution to remain steadfast in its
relation with God.

In the third mansion, God withdraws spiritual sweetness from
the soul, so that it may experience aridity. The person at this
stage has been aptly described as "the good adult Christian,"
that is to say, one who is living a well-ordered, decent,

Christian life.[10] However, this life may be very secure, so secure that it borders on a spiritual complacency. There is need for more. The purpose is to enable the soul to grow in humility, conforming itself to Christ by accepting willingly its sufferings. This stage demands total renunciation.

The fourth mansion witnesses the deeper relation of the soul with God, in which it experiences the favor of consolations. Special vigilance is necessary here because "as the natural is united with the supernatural . . . it is here that the devil can do the most harm; for in the dwelling places of which I have not yet spoken the Lord gives him fewer opportunities" (4, 3, 15). In the fifth mansion, God bestows the favor of the Prayer of Union, perhaps accompanied by intense experiences of God's presence (see 5, 1, 9).

In the sixth and seventh mansions Teresa uses the comparison of betrothal and marriage to describe what happens between the soul and God. In the sixth mansion, the "soul is now completely determined to take no other spouse; but the Spouse disregards its yearnings for the conclusion of the betrothal, desiring that they should become still deeper and that this greatest of all blessings should be won by the soul at some cost to itself" (6, 1, 1). The suffering, trial and perhaps even persecutions that occur are further invitations to be conformed to the Christ who suffered for us. At the same time, the soul experiences great graces and favors from God. In the seventh mansion the soul is united with God in the spiritual marriage.

In more traditional language, mansions 1–3 have to do with the "purgative way," mansion 4 with the "illuminative way," and mansions 5–7 with the "unitive way."[11] This mystical union with God, the vision and understanding of the Trinity, is described well by one commentator as a "breaking through of fragmented visions of God to an actual living in the Trinity."[12] It distressed Teresa that so few Christians seemed interested in this contemplative way that led to union with God. She wrote: "It's a great shame, and quite distressing that, by our own fault, we don't understand ourselves, or know who we are."[13]

Church

Dying, Teresa said: "Finally, Lord, I am a daughter of the Church."[14] This attitude was hers throughout life, a strong sense of attachment to the Church. According to Teresa, the signs of love consist in this:

> In desiring with strong determination to please God in everything, in striving, insofar as possible, not to offend him, and in asking him for the advancement of the honor and glory of his Son and the increase of the Catholic Church.[15]

In fact, her first foundation, St. Joseph in Avila, was to be a house of "unceasing prayer" to serve a Church torn apart by the Reformation.[16] Keith Egan summarizes this devotion of Teresa to the Church: "Teresa of Jesus . . . and the women who follow her are daughters of the Church whose very raison d'être is to meet the need of the Church. Teresa spends the rest of her life and all her energy extending this ecclesial commitment by means of her subsequent foundations."[17]

She extends this ecclesial commitment also through her writings, but in each of them she is careful to submit everything to the authority and teaching of the Church. After the Council of Trent there was a growing awareness of the Church's institutional dimension and the need for reform. This too is part of Teresa's life and awareness, but she never gets lost in institutionalism. She has a theocentric and christocentric view of the Church, nicely described by Keith Egan: "For Teresa the Church is 'God's Church.' More specifically, the Church is Christ."[18]

Teresa's central image for the Church is the Church as Mother. Needless to say, this image is not peculiar to her. It has distinguished lineage, going back through the patristic period into the New Testament, and it occurs in her contemporaries, John of the Cross and Ignatius of Loyola, as well as in the Council of Trent.[19] It is Teresa's sense of being a daughter of the Church that affords our lead-in to understanding the place of the Eucharist in her life. It was not extraordinary, in the sense of being conceptually different from the average informed Catholic of the day; but its sheer ordinariness remains its very strength.

Eucharist

We will not find Teresa of Avila in any of the standard histories of eucharistic theology or spirituality. There are at least two major reasons for this. First, her eucharistic understanding was not significantly different from that of her Catholic counterparts throughout Europe. A renewal was afoot. She was part of it. But the renewers/reformers in the Catholic camp would have shared, all else being equal, the understanding of the Council of Trent. In respect of the Eucharist, the council fathers at Trent did not see themselves as innovators, but as repeating creatively the tradition which they had received. They repeated this antique eucharistic faith in response to the Reformers, most especially Huldrych Zwingli, whose understanding of the Eucharist was significantly different.[20] It is a well-known fact that Teresa had no love for what she understood of the Reformers, and so her eucharistic faith would have been the common eucharistic faith of Catholics. Second, for that very reason the Eucharist would have been central to her spirituality, for it was at the heart of the Church. If one were to say that in Teresian spirituality the Eucharist is taken for granted, that is a positive statement. It was assumed that in any form of orthodox Catholicism the Eucharist would be central. Indeed, one could maintain that if Teresa's eucharistic theology and spirituality had been in any degree deviant from the Catholic norm, we would have explicit knowledge of it. As the Anglican ecclesiastical historian David L. Edwards puts it, "Their [Teresa and John of the Cross] sanctity included an indisputable orthodoxy and thus they escaped the worst wrath of the Inquisition, the organization which arrested the country's most senior bishop on charges of heresy."[21] We will not find in *La Madre,* the Mother, as she was called, the eloquent eucharistic testimony of a Hildegard, Hadewijch, Mechthild or Julian. What we shall discover is the ordinary Catholic appreciation of the Eucharist as central.

The problem, if that is the right word, lies in Teresa's mysticism. The very word "mysticism" has attached to it a grandiose and paranormal meaning at the popular level. People expect the mystic to be someone who has a facility or aptitude for wondrous experiences that originate in the powers of the subject. One of the problems of the word "mysticism" (and its cognates) in modern parlance is that it is understood to be a state of consciousness, albeit a remarkable state of consciousness, which can be to some degree plotted and charted. It may even be that someone like Teresa contributed to this understanding by providing generations to follow with an account of her own experiences. But to leave mysticism at this level of understanding is to fail to do justice to Teresa.

For her, mysticism is the working out, the articulation, the expression of what is involved in union with Christ. Says Bishop Rowan Williams, "If we take away or water down her Christological framework, with its corporate and ecclesial, moral and sacramental dimensions, what is left appears all too easily as a schema of psychic adventure, an unprecedentedly full and, above all, continuous record of mystical experience."[22] The Protestant systematic theologian Jurgen Moltmann makes similar remarks in his comparison of Teresa and Luther:

> What holds Teresa so indivisibly fast to Christ is not the thought of the image, which one uses in meditation and leaves behind in contemplation, but rather the experience of the Eucharist. The body and blood of Christ in bread and wine — broken and shed for us — this is for her the humanity of Christ.[23]

It is not thinking about Christ that brings about union with Christ, though it must be said that such meditation can never be unimportant for a Christian. It is the ontology that comes through the Eucharist that is the thing. It is a bonding into union with Christ through the bonding offered by Christ himself.

In *The Way of Perfection* Teresa offers us a commentary on the Lord's Prayer. "Give us this day our daily bread" reminds her of the Eucharist.

> His majesty gave us . . . the manna and nourishment of his humanity that we might find him at will and not die of hunger, save through our own fault. In no matter how many ways the soul may desire to eat, it will find delight and consolation in the most Blessed Sacrament.[24]

Her deep faith in the Eucharist led to the healing of illness as she experienced it in her own person.[25] She writes:

> Now, then, if when he went about in the world the mere touch of his robes cured the sick, why doubt, if we have faith, that miracles will be worked while he is within us, and that he will give what we ask of him, since he is within our house. His Majesty is not accustomed to paying poorly for his lodging if the hospitality is good.[26]

Teresa's visions were often "triggered by moments of intense petition or by reception of the Eucharist."[27]

Conclusion

Three of the women in this book have been made Doctors of the Church: Catherine of Siena, Teresa of Avila and Therese of Lisieux. In his homily at the Mass for the proclamation of the doctorate of Teresa of Avila, Pope Paul VI said: "We have conferred — rather we have acknowledged — St. Teresa of Jesus' title of Doctor of the Church."[28] The acknowledgment of

Teresa of Avila

Teresa's doctorate has to do with her mystical theology, her grasp of the lineaments of the mystical life, in union with the Trinity. But, if the Eucharist is necessarily at the center of life, and Teresa lived this Catholic life to the full, may we not legitimately say also that her doctorate has to do with her ordinary appreciation of the Eucharist? One could put it in another way. Would her mystical experience have been possible without the Eucharist? I think not. Margaret Brennan, in an essay on Teresa's spirituality, ends with these words:

> To be able to discern the word and action of God's Spirit in our own time requires that we be rooted in the best traditions of our past, but it also demands that our own lives be so in touch with God that we can trust the deepest desires of our own hearts in charting a future not yet clear to us.[29]

Perhaps what we discern in Teresian eucharistic spirituality is not some insight about the Eucharist peculiar to her, but simply its being there, tacitly but really as the very center of life. If that is true of Teresa, may it not also be true of us?

1   For comparison and contrast between Teresa and Luther see Jurgen Moltmann, "Teresa of Avila and Martin Luther," *Studies in Religion*, 13, 1984, pp. 265–78, and Donald C. Nugent, "What has Wittenberg to Do with Avila? Martin Luther and St. Teresa," *Journal of Ecumenical Studies*, 23, 1986, pp. 650–58.

2   *Women Mystics*, (tr. A. E. Nash), San Francisco: Ignatius Press, 1993, pp. 87–92.

3   Rowan Williams, *Teresa of Avila*, London: Geoffrey Chapman, 1991, p. 13.

4   Tr. and ed. by E. Allison Peers, New York and London: Doubleday, 1946.

5   *Teresa of Avila, The Interior Castle*, tr. Kieran Kavanaugh, O.C.D., and Otilio Rodriguez, O.C.D., New York-Ramsey-Toronto: Paulist Press, 1979.

6   *The Collected Works of St. Teresa of Avila*, tr. Kieran Kavanaugh, O.C.D., and Otilio Rodriguez, O.C.D., vol. 1: *The Book of Her Life, Spiritual Testimonies, Soliloquies*, Washington DC: ICS Publications, 1976.

7   *Life*, 8, 5.

8   *Life*, 40, 8, cited in Keith J. Egan, "Teresa of Jesus, Daughter of the Church and Woman of the Reformation," in John Sullivan, O.C.D., ed., *Centenary of St. Teresa*, (Carmelite Studies), Washington DC: ICS Publications, 1984, p. 72.

9   John Welch, O.Carm., "No Castles in the Air! The Wisdom of Teresa of Avila," *Listening*, 26, 1991, p. 222.

10 Ibid., p. 227.

11 E.W. Trueman Dicken, "Teresa of Avila and John of the Cross," in Cheslyn Jones, Geoffrey Wainwright and Edward Yarnold, S.J., ed., *The Study of Spirituality*, London: S.P.C.K., 1986, p. 375.

12 Gillian T. W. Ahlgren, *Teresa of Avila and the Politics of Sanctity*, Ithaca and London: Cornell University Press, 1996, p. 86. See also p. 105.

13 *The Interior Castle*, 1, 1, 2.

Teresa of Avila

[14] Egan, op. cit. p. 69.

[15] *The Interior Castle,* 4, 1, 7.

[16] *The Way of Perfection,* 4, 1.

[17] Egan, op. cit., p. 73.

[18] Ibid., p. 79.

[19] Ibid., p. 80.

[20] See the chapter, "The Reformers and Eucharistic Ecclesiology," in Owen F. Cummings, *Eucharistic Soundings,* Dublin: Veritas Publications, 1999.

[21] David L. Edwards, *Christianity: The First Two Thousand Years,* Maryknoll NY: Orbis Books, 1997, p. 338.

[22] Williams, op. cit., p. 148.

[23] Moltmann, op. cit., p. 272, his emphasis.

[24] *The Way of Perfection,* 34.2.

[25] Eamon R. Carroll, O.Carm., "The Saving Role of the Human Christ for St. Teresa," in John Sullivan, O.C.D., op. cit., p. 147.

[26] *The Way of Perfection,* 34.8.

[27] Ahlgren, op. cit., p. 102. See *Life,* 28.1, 3.

[28] Cited in Keith J. Egan, "The Significance for Theology of the Doctor of the Church: Teresa of Avila," in Robert Masson, ed., *The Pedagogy of God's Image,* Chico CA: Scholars Press, 1982, p. 161.

[29] "Teresa of Avila: 'Undaunted Daughter of Desire,'" in Annice Callahan, R.S.C.J., ed., *Spiritualities of the Heart,* Mahwah NJ: Paulist Press, 1990, p. 128.

Chapter 9

Therese of Lisieux

"**A** saint," says Lawrence Cunningham, "is a person so grasped by a religious vision that it becomes central to his or her life in a way that radically changes the person and leads others to glimpse the value of that vision."[1] The definition of Cunningham's is undoubtedly true of all saints, but it is most apt for Saint Therese of Lisieux. She had a religious vision, though to her it seemed so very ordinary, and after her death this vision caught the imagination of millions of people, not only Catholics. Recently, a fine appreciative and creative essay on Therese has appeared from the pen of the Anglican systematic theologian and Regius Professor of Divinity at the University of Cambridge, David F. Ford.[2] One thinks also of the interest of earlier generations of Anglicans, Monsignors Vernon Johnson and Ronald Knox. Johnson began as a Franciscan in the Anglican tradition and, after becoming Catholic, spent about 30 years dedicating himself to the spread of Therese's "Little Way," especially among priests. Knox was later to translate her biography into English. Therese's very popularity, however, has become something of a problem because of the sheer volume of literature to which she has given rise, not all of it valuable. As Louis Bouyer comments, it is "more discouraging than inspiring."[3]

Life and Spirituality

Marie Francoise Therese Martin was born at Alençon, Normandy, on January 2, 1873, the ninth and youngest child of Louis Martin and Zelie Guerin. Four of the five children who lived beyond childhood became Carmelite nuns in the convent at Lisieux, the city to which the family moved after Zelie's death in 1877. From the age of five Therese lived in Lisieux where she entered the Carmelite monastery when she was only fifteen, receiving the religious name of Sister Therese of the Child Jesus and the Holy Face. Her education was poor both "on the religious plane and on the plane of simple humanity," yet Therese was able to develop not only a healthy spirituality but also a most attractive spirituality.[4] The asceticism of the Carmel was not for Therese a negative way, a way of denial and death for its own sake. It was understood as "the condition of growth and transformation," and, as Noel D. O'Donoghue, O.D.C., points out, the family was not tinged by Jansenism: "It is important to remember that the Martins were not Jansenists. Indeed, if anything, they were anti-Jansenistic in their emphasis on love rather than fear, in their practical belief in frequent communion, in their sense of fun and celebration."[5] After her brief life in the cloister, completely unknown, she died September 30, 1897, at the young age of twenty-four. The custom among the Carmelites was to send other Carmels a brief biography of each sister who had passed away; so, under obedience, Therese had written her own spiritual autobiography before her death. In 1898, as was the custom, this was passed around, but it went well beyond the Carmelite world and had an immediate impact.

"Therese seemed in Carmel only remarkable in her simplicity and ordinariness."[6] Before she died, she said on July 16 to her sister, Mother Agnes, "I feel my mission is soon to begin, my mission to teach souls my little way." When Mother Agnes asked what she meant by this, Therese replied, "It is the way of spiritual childhood, the way of trust and absolute surrender." She went on to explain this "little way" at some length:

> It means that we acknowledge our nothingness;
> that we expect everything from the good Lord, as a
> child expects everything from its father; it means
> to worry about nothing, seeking only to gather
> flowers, the flowers of sacrifices, and to offer them
> to the good Lord for his pleasure. It also means not
> to attribute to ourselves the virtues we practise,
> not to believe we are capable of anything, but to
> acknowledge that it is the good Lord who has

placed that treasure in the hand of his little child
that he may use it when he needs it, but it remains
always God's own treasure. Finally, it means that
we must not be discouraged by our faults, for children fall frequently.

This notion of "spiritual infancy" is not new, and is in fact one
of the major themes of the French School in the seventeenth
century. It reaches, however, its supreme expression in the
"Little Way" of Saint Therese.[7]

Therese also speaks in her *Story of a Soul* of having to put up
with a great "trial of faith." As she describes this trial, she
speaks of "the timid glimmerings of the dawn . . . [giving] way
to the burning heat of noon," of her soul "invaded by the
thickest darkness." One commentator has compared this dark
experience of Therese to the existential nothingness articulated by the philosophers of the mid-twentieth century: "It is
[Therese] herself who used a phrase that Heidegger or Sartre
might have used thirty years later: *la nuit de neant,* the night
of nothingness."[8] It was an experience almost of annihilation.

At the same time she said, "God was enlightening my soul"
and "giving me even the experience of years." This com-
pressed enlightenment, the gift of God, is to the effect that
now she has deeper insight into the reality of Jesus: "Never
have I felt before . . . how sweet and merciful the Lord really
is. . . . God has given me the grace to understand what charity is." The command of Jesus leaps into life for her: "A new
commandment I give to you, that you love one another; even
as I have loved you, that you also love one another. By this all
men will know that you are my disciples, if you have love for
one another" (John 13:34–35). And now Therese wants to love
"to the point of dying love," to "be broken through love," as
Jesus was. The entire paschal event of Jesus has become
luminously clear to her, through her experience of darkness,
this "trial of faith," as the very mystery of divine love. Her
insight yields "a metaphysic of charity" leading us "to par-

ticipate in building a civilization of love in human history."[9] The theologian William M. Thompson puts this experience of Therese, from the dark night to the vision of love, in these fine words: "If we follow Therese's clue, the mystical dark night, at least on one of its levels, is a plunge into the ocean of radically selfless love."[10]

Therese also took as part of her "name in religion" the devotion to "the Holy Face." How is this to be understood? Immediately it conjures up the suffering Face of Jesus on the *via dolorosa,* the face wiped by Veronica, the face on the Shroud of Turin. O'Donoghue comments, "It is indeed moving to see how Therese's own countenance, in successive photographs, takes on something of the image of the crucified, as if her whole being reflected her beloved ever more deeply."[11] Her growth into Christ is accompanied by a physical likeness to Christ. At the same time it comes after "of the Child Jesus." This establishes a certain wholism in her spiritual understanding. Thompson believes that Therese indicates by this "her christological relevance: it is Jesus she will try to exemplify, but inclusively, from childhood through the passion [the Holy Face/Shroud]."[12] In a sense her entire person was configured to Christ, because she remained childlike and through her later suffering participated in the face of Christ's sufferings.

Eucharist

There is a wonderful passage in *Story of a Soul* where Therese tells of her "desire" to be a priest:

> I feel in me the vocation of the priest. With what love, O Jesus, I would carry You in my hands when, at my voice, You would come down from heaven. And with what love would I give You to souls! But alas! While desiring to be a priest, I admire and envy the humility of Saint Francis of Assisi and I feel the vocation of imitating him in refusing the sublime dignity of the priesthood.[13]

Therese of Lisieux

What is noticeable about the passage is the reason for her desire to be a priest: in order to bring the eucharistic Christ to people. In that sense, the priesthood for her is secondary to the primary reality of the Eucharist. Then, after meditating on 1 Corinthians 13, the "hymn to love," she writes:

> Charity gave me the key to my vocation. . . . I understood that the Church had a heart and that this heart was burning with love. . . . I understood that love comprised all vocations, that love was everything, that it embraced all times and places. . . . In a word, that it was eternal! Then, in the excess of my delirious joy, I cried out: O Jesus, my Love . . . my vocation, at last I have found it. . . . My vocation is Love! . . . Thus I shall be everything, and thus my dream will be realized.[14]

It is not in the least degree fanciful, given Therese's love for the sacrament, to see the Eucharist at the very center of this vision. As a child, she had the custom of making regular visits with her father to the Blessed Sacrament. She loved to participate in processions of the Blessed Sacrament, strewing flowers in front of the monstrance.

In Therese's time daily communion was not a common practice, and so not open to her as a religious. More frequent reception of the Eucharist had to wait until Pope Pius X lowered the age for initial reception, and encouraged frequent reception. That would not happen until 1905. Nonetheless, she used every opportunity to approach the Eucharist.[15] The superior of the convent, Mother Mary Gonzague, stayed with the strict interpretation of the religious rule: communion only once a week. This was a real trial for Therese. In 1890 Pope Leo XIII transferred the right of prescribing the frequency of reception to the chaplains of religious communities; that eased matters for her to some extent.

She experiences the Eucharist as a means of her "christification," her deification in Christ. "Therese had learned that there is no more efficacious means of transforming ourselves into Jesus than the worthy reception of Christ's Sacred Body."[16] She expresses this conviction of the tradition poetically:

> Thy spouse am I, thy chosen one.
> My well-beloved, come, dwell in me.
> Oh come! Thy beauty wins my heart.
> Deign to transform me into Thee.[17]

That last line, "Deign to transform me into Thee," expresses a motif of this book, that the Eucharist makes the Church. The Eucharist is the Christ-given means of our deification.

During the last weeks of her life, Therese was unable to receive holy communion. Just over one month before she died, Therese's sister Pauline realized that she feared to receive the Eucharist lest she would choke and vomit. Pauline described the situation of August 20, 1897, in these words: "That day she was unable to restrain herself any longer and she fell into tears . . . the choking produced by her sobs was so violent that, not only was she unable to answer us, but she made a sign to us not to say a word, not even to look at her. . . . Never had I seen her in such agony."[18] This description by Pauline is just one day after Therese's last communion. From the agony described, one gets some minute glimpse of just what the Eucharist meant to Therese.

In the "Act of Oblation" which she had made on June 9, 1895, Therese had said, "I cannot receive Holy Communion as often as I desire, but, dear Lord, are You not omnipotent? . . . Remain within me as in the tabernacle."[19] Some sacramental theologians today may find this expression lacking; it may to some appear to give a priority to the reserved sacrament over the received sacrament. This would be to overlook the times, times when the frequent reception of communion was far from encouraged. The tabernacle is for Therese, as for all

Catholics of her time, *the* symbol of the eucharistic presence of Christ. Therefore, she wishes to be what the tabernacle is, that is, the place of Christ, the place where Christ remains.

There is a further theological insight in this expression of Therese's about "remaining within me as in the tabernacle," to do with an appreciation of the "real presence." One could argue that the tabernacle is a necessary expression of Catholic belief in the real, eucharistic presence of Christ. In a sense, the tabernacle with the reserved sacrament acts as a reminder to the eucharistic community that, while it is an incarnational expression of the body of Christ, that expression is not and cannot be complete until the end, the *parousia*. As Francis Mannion put it, "A church that regards itself as the body of Christ without qualification suffers from a collapsed eschatology and ultimately an impoverished self-understanding. By the same token, when the eschatological factor of the eucharist is appropriately symbolized, the church is being drawn beyond itself to the fullness of being to be realized only at the heavenly banquet."[20]

Now clearly Therese did not think quite in this way, but it seems to me that her way of reflecting about the tabernacle was not alien to her thought, nor her thought to this way of thinking. We are the body of Christ especially through the regular reception of holy communion, but the most complete expression of our identity as the body of Christ remains in the future. The tabernacle reminds us of this.

Apparently Therese said to her eldest sister, Sister Marie du Sacre Coeur, concerning the rules that governed the reception of communion, "You will see, when I get to heaven, there will be a change in the Church's practice regarding holy communion."[21] Therese died in 1897. In 1910 Pope Pius X lowered the age for first communion in his decree *Quam singulari;* he was also in the forefront of encouraging frequent communion.

She comes to the aid of the scrupulous, whose sense of unworthiness keeps them from the sacrament. In a letter to Marie Guerin on May 30, 1889, Therese wrote:

> When the devil has succeeded in keeping a soul away from holy communion, he has gained all . . . and Jesus weeps! O my darling, do you realize that Jesus is there in the tabernacle expressly for you — for you alone. He burns with the desire to come into your heart . . . don't listen to the demon, laugh at him, and go without fear to receive the Jesus of peace and love. . . . Dearest little Sister, receive communion often, very often . . . there you have the sole remedy, if you want to be cured. Jesus has not put this attraction into your heart for nothing."[22]

Conclusion

Pope John Paul II declared Therese of Lisieux Doctor of the Church on October 16, 1997. The declaration is most instructive. Therese did not have higher degrees in theology, nor was she engaged in the exploration and explanation of the sacred mysteries. She did not publish any books on the meaning of Christian doctrine. Christopher O'Donnell, the Irish Carmelite, captures the sense in which we may rightly describe Therese as a theologian: "It is not through academic research, but through being taught directly by God in and through love."[23] This certainly seems to be the meaning of Pope John Paul II in his homily preached in October 1997, on the occasion of Therese's being named Doctor of the Church. The pope said, "Therese of Lisieux did not only grasp and describe the profound truth of love as the center and heart of the Church, but in her short life she lived it intensely. It is precisely this convergence of doctrine and concrete experience, of truth and life, of teaching and practice, which shines with particular brightness in this saint, and which makes her an attractive model especially for young people and for those who are seeking true meaning for their life."[24] Therese's witness consists in living her theology and articulating her life in

Therese of Lisieux

Story of a Soul. The center of that living and that articulation was the Eucharist.

1   Lawrence S. Cunningham, *The Meaning of Saints,* San Francisco: Harper and Row, 1980, p. 65.

2   David F. Ford, "Before the Face of Christ," *The Way,* 37, 1997, pp. 154–262. The essay is reproduced in his creative *Self and Salvation, Being Transformed,* Cambridge: Cambridge University Press, 1999, pp. 216–40.

3   Louis Bouyer, *Women Mystics,* (tr. A. E. Nash), San Francisco: Ignatius Press, 1993, p. 132.

4   Ibid., p. 134.

5   Noel D. O'Donoghue, O.D.C., "Cloister and Cosmos: St. Therese of Lisieux," in his *Mystics for Our Time,* Wilmington DE: Michael Glazier, 1989, p. 116. See also Christopher O'Donnell, O.Carm., *Love in the Heart of the Church, The Mission of Therese of Lisieux,* Dublin: Veritas Publications, 1997, p. 24 and Stephane Joseph Piat, O.F.M., "Saint of the Eucharist," in Brother Francis Mary, F.I., ed., *St. Therese, Doctor of the Little Way,* New Bedford MA: Our Lady's Chapel, 1997, p. 148.

6   Michael Hollings, "Therese of Lisieux," in Gordon S. Wakefield, ed., *A Dictionary of Christian Spirituality,* London: SCM Press, 1983, p. 377.

7   John Saward, "Berulle and the French School," in Cheslyn Jones, Geoffrey Wainwright and Edward Yarnold, S.J., ed., *The Study of Spirituality,* London: S.P.C.K., 1986, p. 392.

8   Noel D. O'Donoghue, O.D.C., op. cit., p. 122.

9   These are the expressions of the International Theological Commission, *Theology, Christology, Anthropology,* Washington DC: U.S.C.C., 1983, pp. 10–11.

10 William M. Thompson, *Fire and Light: The Saints and Theology,* New York and Mahwah: Paulist Press, 1987, p. 92. See also Bouyer, op. cit., pp. 143–44.

11 O'Donoghue, op. cit., p. 119.

12 William M. Thompson, *Christology and Spirituality,* New York: Crossroad, 1991, p. 127.

13 *Story of a Soul,* 3d ed., tr. John Clarke, O.C.D., Washington DC: ICS Publications, 1996, p. 192.

14 Ibid., p. 194.

15 Francois Jamart, O.C.D., *Complete Spiritual Doctrine of St. Therese of Lisieux,* (tr. W. Van De Putte), New York: Alba House, 1961, p. 269.

16 Ibid.

17 Cited in Piat, op. cit., p. 150.

18 *St. Therese of Lisieux: Her Last Conversations,* cited in Patricia O'Connor, *In Search of Therese,* Wilmington DE: Michael Glazier, 1987, pp. 59–60.

19 Ibid., p. 150.

20 M. Francis Mannion, "The Reserved Eucharist," *Antiphon, A Journal for Liturgical Renewal,* 3, 1998, p. 3.

21 Ibid., p. 151.

22 Ibid., p. 153.

23 O'Donnell, op. cit., p. 211.

24 Cited in Francis Mary, op. cit., p. 70.

Thérèse of the Child Jesus and the Holy Face
living in Christ's mystical body
with two of her sisters, *from left,*
Pauline Martin as Mother Agnes of Jesus and
Céline Martin as Sister Geneviève of the Holy Faith, and a cousin
Marie Guérin as Sister Maria of the Eucharist,
all Discalced Carmelites of Lisieux, France

Thérèse Martin, youngest of nine children, was born in Alençon in 1873, and a year after this photo was taken she died at Lisieux in 1896 at 24. Popularly known as the Little Flower, she was declared patron of France as well as a saint, virgin and doctor of the Church. In her autobiography she focused on the "little way" of suffering and rejoicing with Jesus. She saw her life as a mystic song gratitude to Christ whom she found present with her in every experience. We celebrate her memory on October 1.

Edith Stein in 1921 celebrating life with her cousin Richard in Göttingen, Germany
A Jewish woman
philosopher, teacher, author
baptized in the Father, the Son and the Holy Spirit
Discalced Carmelite Sister Teresa Benedicta of the Cross
Holocaust victim

Born in Breslau on Yom Kippur of 1891, Edith Stein was first a proud daughter of the God of Israel and then a proud daughter of the God of Israel and Christians, dying a martyr at Auschwitz in 1942 for love of that God. She celebrated Christian initiation in Göttingen on January 1, 1921, entered the Carmel of Cologne, Germany, in 1933 and was forced to flee in 1938 to the Carmel of Echt, Holland. Arrested there with her sister Rosa, Edith was executed in the gas chambers on August 9, 1942. Pope John Paul II beatified her in 1987 and canonized her in 1998. We celebrate her memory August 9.

Chapter 10

Edith Stein

Saint Edith Stein makes an interesting contrast with Saint Therese of Lisieux: Edith was born into a Jewish family; Therese was a cradle Catholic. Edith, the doctor in philosophy; Therese, ill educated but later Doctor of the Church; both daughters of the Carmel; both to die prematurely: Therese of tuberculosis and Edith gassed at Auschwitz.

Edith Stein was born in Breslau, Silesia (now in Poland), on October 12, 1891, the daughter of Siegfried and Augusta Stein.[1] She was born on the Jewish feast of Yom Kippur, the Day of Atonement; apparently, her mother often mentioned this fact, and Edith grew up with a sense of specialness because of it.[2] Her father died at age 48, leaving her mother not only to raise the children but also to manage a failing lumber yard. As the youngest child of the family, Edith's bond with her mother was "the strongest emotional bond in her life."[3] She termed herself an atheist, unable to pray, a situation that lasted through her studies at the University of Breslau and the University of Gottingen; she began to attend the latter in 1913, to study under the German philosopher, Edmund Husserl. Husserl was the center of a philosophical circle of Jewish intellectuals who had become Christian, including Adolf Reinach and Max Scheler. The witness of these men was to have a significant impact on this young, atheistic Jewish philosopher. Her doctoral thesis in philosophy under Husserl was entitled *On the Problem of Empathy.* "Empathy" is best described as "not only a sympathy necessary to an authentic understanding of what one is studying but an effort to place oneself literally within the object studied."[4]

She taught for a short time at the high school in Breslau, but in 1916 she followed Husserl to the University of Freiburg as his assistant; she remained there for eighteen months. In 1917 her friend Adolf Reinach was killed at the front during the course of World War I. Edith went to pay her condolences to Reinach's widow. "To her surprise she found a woman at peace rather than a despairing widow. Anna was able to stand up to the blow because of her strong Christian faith."[5] The example of Anna Reinach was a powerful factor in Edith's making her own way into the Christian faith. Her spiritual struggles did not cease yet. She left her academic post with Edmund Husserl in 1918 and returned to Breslau, where she continued to write. In 1921, while at a philosopher friend's house, a sort of vast estate in which guests could spend time in meditative retreat, Edith picked up and read right through Teresa of Avila's autobiography. She bought a catechism, a missal and, soon after, a breviary. Whenever she was in Breslau, Edith accompanied her mother to the synagogue, where she followed the psalms in her breviary.[6] On January 1, 1922, she was baptized at St. Martin's Church in Bergzabern.

Her life changed radically. She lived a very active life praying the Divine Office and participating fully in the liturgy. She spent eight years teaching in a Dominican school in Speyer. Her life was taking the obvious shape of a vowed religious. Through a disciple of Husserl, Dietrich Von Hildebrand, Edith was introduced to the Jesuit philosopher-theologian Erich Przywara; it was he who guided her into the work of John Henry Cardinal Newman and Saint Thomas Aquinas. She steeped herself in theology, translating into German some of Newman's work and Aquinas's *On Truth*, as well as continuing to write philosophy. She then became familiar with the Benedictines at Beuron, and particularly with their abbot, Raphael Walzer. From 1928 until she entered the Cologne Carmel, Edith spent every Holy Week in Beuron. Her love of the liturgy now deepened and expanded. As a result she wrote an essay entitled "The Prayer of the Church." The gist of the essay is that the center of the prayer of the Church is the Eucharist, itself the memorial of the cross, prepared for in

prayer and extended in prayer.[7] Because of her growing reputation as a speaker, she left her teaching post at Speyer in 1931.

She attempted to obtain a teaching post in philosophy at the
University of Freiburg, but without success. Her former fel-
low student and colleague, Martin Heidegger, now held a chair
of philosophy at Freiburg. Freda Oben commented, "In fact,
[Edith] felt herself treated by him with considerable ill will.
This is not surprising in light of the fact that at the time
Heidegger was a strong supporter of the Nazis."[8] Later,
Heidegger was to publish under his own name some of the
manuscripts of Husserl that Edith herself had worked on.[9]
Eventually, she found a post in 1932 at the German Institute for
Scientific Pedagogy, attached to the University of Munster.
But 1932 was only one year before the Nazi ascendancy in
Germany. Hitler came to power on January 30, 1933, and
Edith's position became impossible. Her last lecture was deliv-
ered on February 25. She wrote of her last days in Munster,
"Now of a sudden it was luminously clear to me that once
again God's hand lay heavy on his people, and that the destiny
of this people was my own."[10]

Later that year, on October 14, 1933, the eve of the feast of
Saint Teresa of Avila, Edith entered the Carmel in Cologne.
Her religious name was Teresia Benedicta a Cruce, Teresa
Blessed by the Cross.

Edith's mother found her conversion very difficult to understand, and it may have seemed to her almost a betrayal of her
Judaism at a time in Germany when the evil logic of Hitler's
anti-Semitism was starting to unfold. Edith, of course, knew
of her mother's hurt and of the suspicion and distrust sur-
rounding her decision to become a Carmelite. After her mother's death she wrote from the Carmel of Cologne on October
31, 1938, about her family's sufferings as they tried to emigrate
from Germany: "If only [my family] knew where to go! But I
trust that, from eternity, Mother will take care of them. And [I
also trust] in the Lord's having accepted my life for all of

them. I keep having to think of Queen Esther who was taken from among her people precisely so that she might represent them before the king. I am a very poor and powerless little Esther, but the King who chose me is infinitely great and merciful. That is such a great comfort."[11] In a similar vein she had written in a letter of May 14, 1934, to Fritz Kaufmann, another Jewish student from her time at Gottingen with whom she had not been in touch for some years: "Whoever enters Carmel is not lost to her own, but is theirs fully for the first time; it is our vocation to stand before God for all."[12] It would be fair to say that her sense of embodiment in Christ, and of radical vocation in Christ as a Carmelite, gave her this profound sense of being connected through that embodiment-vocation to her immediate family, to her Jewish sisters and brothers, and ultimately to the entire family of God. It was a sense that one person is no person, so to speak, but rather that all are inter-connected in Christ, so that the good done by one benefits all.

Edith remained in Cologne as Sister Teresia Benedicta a Cruce until her superior judged it too dangerous for her to remain. During her time there she continued to study and write. One of her most significant books, *Finite and Eternal Being*, was written at this time but could not be published because of Nazi policy. Another fine book, *The Science of the Cross,* in which she explores the meaning of the Cross of Christ through the understanding of Saint John of the Cross, again came from her Carmelite period. Steven Payne, O.C.D., makes an insightful comment here that is of significance for all concerned with theology: "It is a striking fact that Edith's most important works, like all the great Carmelite classics, were written not within the protective environment of a university campus but in the midst of a religious community, with its constant demands and interruptions. In a sense we can see her as a model for the many women and men who have to pursue scholarship and find their voice outside the customary academic channels."[13] Payne is right, and Edith's example and his words will give hope to many theologians who serve the Church, but not in the academy.

Edith's superiors arranged for her transfer to the Carmel in Echt, Holland, on New Year's Eve in 1938, along with her sister Rosa, who had also converted to Catholicism. Edith feared for the safety of her Carmelite sisters as much as they feared for hers. Their safety at Echt was short-lived. On August 2, 1942, as a response to the Dutch bishops' protest against the persecution of the Jews, all the Jewish Catholics in Holland were arrested, including Edith and Rosa. They were taken to Auschwitz and executed there on August 9. Almost the last words she spoke as she and her sister were being taken from the Echt Carmel were these: "Come, Rosa, we are going for our people!"[14]

The day of Edith and Rosa's death brings to mind a holy day their mother would have kept: the ninth day of the Jewish month of Ab was a day of fast for Jews in memory of the destruction of the first and second Temples in Jerusalem. "The ninth day of August in the year of 1942 saw the destruction of Edith and Rosa Stein, with countless other temples of the Spirit in the infamy of Auschwitz."[15]

Eucharist

On the wall beside the font of St. Martin's Church where Edith was baptized on January 1, 1922, there is a plaque dedicated to her, outlining the scene from 1 Kings 19:7, where the angel said to Elijah, "Arise and eat, lest the journey overburden you." Freda Oben commented on this plaque: "It is the heavenly bread awaiting Edith at the baptismal font, the Eucharist, which alone enabled her to ascend the Mount Horeb of her life through the gas chamber, where she died for her people and her faith."[16]

There is a passage on the Eucharist in her beautiful essay "The Prayer of the Church":

> Therefore the whole perpetual sacrificial offering
> of Christ — at the cross, in the holy Mass, and in
> the eternal glory of heaven — can be conceived as

a single great thanksgiving — as Eucharist: as gratitude for creation, salvation, and consummation. Christ presents himself in the name of all creation, whose prototype he is and to which he descended to renew it from the inside out and to lead it to perfection.[17]

This same essay contains a fine but brief commentary on the Lord's Prayer:

All that we need to be received into the communion of saints is summed up in the seven petitions of the Our Father, which the Lord did not pray in his own name, but to instruct us. We say it before communion, and when we say it sincerely and from our hearts and receive communion in the proper spirit, it fulfills all our petitions. Communion delivers us from evil, because it cleanses us of sin and gives us peace of heart that takes away the sting of all other "evils." It brings us the forgiveness of past sins and strengthens us in the face of temptations. It is itself the bread of life that we need daily to grow into eternal life. It makes our will an instrument at God's disposal. Thereby it lays the foundation for the kingdom of God in us and gives us clean lips and a pure heart to glorify God's holy name.[18]

Edith shows at times a rich grasp of the interconnection of word and sacrament. In a reflection written for January 6, 1941, she says:

And the same Savior, whom the written word presents to our eyes on all the paths he trod on earth in human form, lives among us disguised in the form of the eucharistic bread. He comes to us every day as the bread of life. In either of these forms he is near to us; in either of these forms he wants to be sought and found by us. The one supports the other. When we see that savior before us with the eyes of faith as the Scriptures portray him, then our desire to receive him in the bread of life increases. The eucharistic bread, on the other hand, awakens our desire to get to know the Lord in the written word more and more deeply and strengthens our spirit to get a better understanding.[19]

In some ways this was to anticipate the eucharistic vision of the Second Vatican Council in the "Constitution on the Sacred Liturgy." In the description of paragraph 7, Christ is present "in the person of His minister," "especially under the Eucharistic species," "in His word" and "when the Church prays and sings." This is, of course, not new in Catholic theology, but in the popular understanding there tended to be an exclusive emphasis of the eucharistic species. Edith does not seem to share that exclusive emphasis.

She speaks of the Carmelite vocation within this context of Christ's presence in her essay, "On the History and Spirit of Carmel":

> [Christ] is present in the most Blessed Sacrament. The hours of adoration before the Highest Good, and listening for the voice of the Eucharistic God, are simultaneously meditation on the Law of the Lord and watching in prayer. But the highest level is reached when the Law is deep within our hearts (Psalm 40:8), when we are so united with the triune God, whose temple we are, that his Spirit rules all we do or omit. . . . To stand before the face of God continues to be the real content of our lives.[20]

In this passage the word "Law" *(Torah,* in Hebrew) means teaching. It is equivalent to God's word, instructing and guiding us. It is as if the Word and Eucharist constitute the central mechanism that enables our standing before the very presence of the triune God. Hence the Carmelite vocation is essentially a eucharistic vocation.

When she speaks to professional women, especially those who are educators, she invites prayer before the Blessed Sacrament:

> [By] informing, educating the young, you lead them into the mysteries of Christ's death and rising, and God's presence in the world. It is by leading them into the mysteries, through the liturgy, that they will be able to deal with the situations of life. . . . It is as nourishing for them to be initiated into the mysteries as it is damaging for them to absorb, uncomprehended, the catechism.[21]

She possesses no naïve view of religious education or catechesis. It must be comprehended according to the age and condition of the person. But she also seems to insinuate that the best catechesis is led by the liturgy, is in fact liturgical catechesis. It is a way of being inducted into the Church's life and meaning through exposure to the sacraments, the liturgical year, the minutiae of custom and ritual that shape our Catholic identity.

She speaks to women specifically about their life as eucharistic:

> A woman's life for which the divine love is to be its inner form, will have to be a eucharistic life. To forget oneself, to be delivered from all one's desires and pretensions, to open one's heart to all the pressing needs of others — this is possible only through the daily intimacy with our Lord in the tabernacle. If we visit the eucharistic God and take counsel with him in all our affairs, if we let ourselves be purified by the sanctifying power that flows from the altar of sacrifice, if we offer ourselves to the Lord in this sacrifice and receive him

into our inmost souls in holy communion, then we
cannot but be drawn ever more deeply into the current of this divine life; we shall grow into the mystical body of Christ, and our heart will be transformed into the likeness of the divine heart.[22]

Admittedly, Edith is speaking this message to women, but
would it not be equally appropriate for men? Perhaps her
meaning is caught by suggesting that traditional male stereo-
types such as domination, control, ratiocination must yield to
the priority of God's grace and so become more receptive and
in that sense more eucharistic. May we even speculate that for
Edith ultimate human maturation takes the form of eucharistic receptivity, and consequently eucharistic transformation,
which receptivity and transformation she sees as specifically
feminine? That a more feminine posture is the paradigm of
what it means to be fully and completely human?

A eucharistic poem composed by Edith brings her eucharistic
reflections to a conclusion:

> Your eyes look deeply into mine with love,
> And to my whispered words you bend your ear.
> You fill my heart with deepest peace.
> And yet your love cannot be satisfied
> By this exchange, for there remains a gap,
> Your heart still asks for more.
> Each morn you come to me at early Mass,
> Your flesh and blood become my food and drink;
> And wonders are accomplished.[23]

Conclusion

As the date of Edith Stein's canonization drew near in 1998,
controversy multiplied. Some argued that it was grossly
insensitive for the Catholic Church to canonize a Jew who had
died in Auschwitz; others, perhaps especially Jews, may see
Edith as a traitor in becoming a Christian. This is an enor-
mously complex and delicate issue, but Hugh Montefiore, the

Edith Stein

former Anglican bishop of Birmingham, England, wrote a letter on the occasion that is worth reading. Montefiore was a Jew who became a Christian; he knows something of Edith's path. He states that few Christians have a real awareness of the treatment of the Jews by Christians over the centuries. "Few Gentile Christians know the details of what happened, but it is firmly lodged in the Jewish folk memory."[24] Montefiore concludes his letter with these words: "Though she had become a Christian, Edith Stein was killed in the Holocaust because she was a Jew: she was a *Jewish* martyr, even if Jews may see her as a traitor. Is it therefore surprising that her canonization, however well-intentioned, may seem a takeover?"[25]

Montefiore's reasoning seems to explain some of the vehement objection that her canonization met. Yet all human beings know in their bones that reconciliation, not domination or takeover, is ultimately what human life is about. Maybe Edith's difficult pilgrimage in both living and dying as a Jewish-Christian, as a Christian-Jew, stands as a permanent invitation to all persons to seek reconciliation for what keeps them apart. For Catholic Christians the primary source of reconciliation is the Eucharist. Edith's pilgrimage was implicitly eucharistic from beginning to end, explicitly eucharistic from the time of her conversion. It was finally eucharistic too as she, steeped in her eucharistic identity, participated in the most intimate way in the paschal mystery through her martyr's death. Edith found herself eschatologically in Christ our Eucharist.

1 For the biographical details I am reliant upon Freda M. Oben, *Edith Stein: Scholar, Feminist, Saint,* New York: Alba House, 1988.

2 James Geoghegan, O.C.D., "St. Edith Stein and the Eucharist," *Carmelite Digest,* 13, 1998, p. 25. I am much indebted to this essay.

3 Steven Payne, O.C.D., "Edith Stein, A Fragmented Life," *America,* 179:10, 1998, p. 12.

4 This description comes from Louis Bouyer, *Women Mystics,* (tr. A. E. Nash), San Francisco: Ignatius Press, 1993, p. 176.

5 Payne, op. cit., p. 15. See also Bouyer, op. cit., p. 177.

6 Ibid., p. 178.

7 An English translation may be found in *The Collected Works of Edith Stein, vol. 4, The Hidden Life,* (tr. W. Stein), Washington DC: ICS Publications, 1992, pp. 7–17.

8 Freda M. Oben, op. cit., pp. 24–25.

Edith Stein

9   Payne, op. cit., p. 12.

10 Cited in Oben, op. cit., p. 26.

11 Cited in Payne, op. cit., p. 13.

12 Ibid.

13 Ibid., pp. 13–14.

14 Ibid., p. 14.

15 L. Gelber and R. Leuven, ed., *Life in a Jewish Family*, (tr. J. Koeppel, O.C.D.), Washington DC: ICS publications, 1986, pp. 441–42.

16 Oben, op. cit., p. 18.

17 L. Gelber and M. Linssen, O.C.D., ed., *The Hidden Life: Essays, Meditations, Spiritual Texts*, Washington DC: ICS Publications, 1992, pp. 89.

18 Ibid., p. 10.

19 Ibid., p. 115.

20 Ibid., p. 4.

21 Cited in Geoghegan, op. cit., p. 28.

22 "The Ethos of Women's Professions," in Hilda Graef, ed., *Writings of Edith Stein*, Westminster MD: The Newman Press, 1956, p. 172.

23 Cited in Geoghegan, op. cit., p. 33.

24 Hugh Montefiore, letter published in *The Tablet*, November 14, 1998, p. 1507.

25 Ibid.

Chapter 11

Conclusion

We have encountered women from Germany, the Netherlands, Italy, England, Spain and France. From Hildegard of Bingen we have received a monastic eucharistic theology, indeed a eucharistic ecclesiology, accompanied by a zeal for the ongoing reform of the Church. From Hadewijch of Antwerp comes a vernacular theology, a sense of intimacy with our eucharistic Lord, of "heart devouring heart." The Cistercian nun, Beatrice of Nazareth, provides us with a "passion for the Eucharist," especially for its healing and deifying dimensions. Mechthild of Magdeburg witnesses to a strong trinitarian eucharistic appreciation and a sense of our human unworthiness. Catherine of Siena bequeaths to us a love for the Church, rooted and grounded in frequent reception of the Eucharist, as Christ "en-worths" us to receive us into himself. The anchoress Julian of Norwich tells us that our Mother Jesus desires to feed us with his own self in the Eucharist, effecting our transformation into him. Catherine of Genoa, overcoming depression and unhappiness in marriage, testifies that in and through the Eucharist — which she could not live without — "My Me is God." Teresa of Avila invites us to personal reformation just as she reformed religious houses sustained by her mystical yet very ordinary appreciation of the reality of the Eucharist. At the beginning of the twentieth century Therese of Lisieux draws us to be tabernacles for the Eucharist, as we pray, "Deign to transform me into Thee." Edith Stein moves from Judaism to Catholicism and from an understanding and love of the eucharistic sacrifice to an absolute performance of that sacrifice in martyrdom at Auschwitz.

That wonderful passage from the letter to the Hebrews comes to mind: "Therefore, since we are surrounded by so great a

Conclusion

cloud of witnesses, let us also lay aside every weight and sin that clings so closely, and let us run with perseverance the race that is set before us, looking to Jesus the pioneer and perfecter of our faith" (Hebrews 12:1–2). This wondrous cloud of witnesses does not merely exemplify for us the depth and range of eucharistic faith and practice. We are most intimately conjoined to them in our own reception of holy communion, as we receive Christ and Christ receives us, the whole Christ, head and members.

In Galatians Saint Paul speaks of our unity in Christ: "For as many of you as were baptized into Christ have put on Christ. There is neither Jew nor Greek, there is neither slave nor free, there is neither male nor female; for you are all one in Christ Jesus" (Galatians 3:27–28). Put into Christ in baptism, we are sustained as his body through the Eucharist. The lives and eucharistic reflections of ten women mystics have been examined in this book. If the past millennium of Christian faith left the eucharistic contribution of women in the margin, the insights of the women treated here, and indeed of countless unknown others, should prevent our making the same mistake in this new millennium.

Index

Index

Index

Index

Index